your VOICE *speaks* volumes

your VOICE *speaks* volumes

it's NOT **WHAT** YOU SAY,
BUT *How You Say It*

Jane SETTER

OXFORD
UNIVERSITY PRESS

OXFORD
UNIVERSITY PRESS

Great Clarendon Street, Oxford, OX2 6DP,
United Kingdom

Oxford University Press is a department of the University of Oxford.
It furthers the University's objective of excellence in research, scholarship,
and education by publishing worldwide. Oxford is a registered trade mark of
Oxford University Press in the UK and in certain other countries

© Jane Setter 2019

The moral rights of the author have been asserted

First Edition published in 2019

Impression: 2

Published in the United States of America by Oxford University Press
198 Madison Avenue, New York, NY 10016, United States of America

British Library Cataloguing in Publication Data
Data available

Library of Congress Control Number: 2019938267

ISBN 978-0-19-881384-2

Printed and bound in Great Britain by
Clays Ltd, Elcograf S.p.A.

Links to third party websites are provided by Oxford in good faith and
for information only. Oxford disclaims any responsibility for the materials
contained in any third party website referenced in this work.

Contents

The companion website at www.oup.co.uk/companion/setter contains useful links, sound files, and colour versions of some images.

CHAPTER 1

The nuts and bolts
How speech works

Have you ever thought about your voice and the way you speak? Really thought about it?

If you're—for example—a singer, a spoken-word performer, have had speech and language therapy, or had an experience which has caused you to use your voice differently, I'll bet you have. But otherwise, unless you've been in a position where someone made some kind of comment about your voice or the way you speak, you may not have thought about it. Even then, you might have just ignored the comment as irrelevant, unimportant, or simply impertinent. But is it?

There is evidence to suggest that the way you speak is just as important now as it ever has been. All sorts of value judgments are made about people on the basis of their voice. The moment you open your mouth and utter that first phrase—no matter what you look like—conclusions are drawn; decisions are made. Some of those conclusions and decisions may have an effect on how successful you are in life.

This book is about the way that people speak and how their voice represents them, both how they perceive it to represent them and the perceptions of others. Among other things, it looks at what influences the way our mother tongue sounds when we speak it, how we can classify and describe speech and accent features, whether the speech of people from different genders is similar or different, what people think accent tells us about speakers and the prejudices people have, how your voice can be used to identify you, how people modify the way they speak (or sing) depending on a variety of factors, and how advances in technology mean that individual voices can now be created for people who can no longer use their own.

The way people speak has always fascinated me, from the sound of the voice itself to the spoken words and grammar. This has probably got a lot to do with my father. Where he'd picked up his Southern British Standard (SBS) accent, I never knew... but he was certainly going to make sure my spoken English didn't descend too far into the local accent and dialect spoken where I grew up. Oh no—that would never do! And so I became fascinated by how people spoke, helped along by my mother's love of Hollywood musicals, and an introduction to the film *My Fair Lady*, which basically seemed to tell my father's story from the point of view of a London flower girl.

'I want to be a lady in a flow'r shop,' says Eliza Doolittle in George Bernard Shaw's play, ''stead of sellin' at the corner of Tottenham Court Road. But they won't take me unless I can talk more genteel.'

And what of Henry Higgins's (male, English-centric) assertion that 'An Englishman's way of speaking absolutely classifies him; the moment he talks, he makes another Englishman despise him'?

As a nation, the British seem to be much more accepting of regional variation than they used to be in, say, the 1950s. If you listen to BBC news and continuity presenters back then, they sound very upper class, usually having what is referred to as a 'cut-glass' accent, or 'The Queen's English'. The official term for the cut-glass accent is 'Received Pronunciation', or 'RP', where 'received' means 'accepted' (more on the subject of RP later). Until fairly recently, regional accents would only appear in fiction or drama on the BBC, not news and current affairs.

These days, there is a variety of accents on the air, and not just confined to regional news programmes. One might assume, therefore, that Henry Higgins's comment no longer applies in this day and age of social mobility. While I have heard tales that in the past BBC broadcasters had received letters complaining about their (usually very mild) regional accents, this seems to be less common nowadays, unless someone has quite a strong regional accent. Recently, BBC Breakfast presenter Steph McGovern, who hails from Middlesbrough and has a discernible Middlesbrough accent (but otherwise speaks with a Standard English dialect whilst on the air), disclosed that a viewer had sent her money for elocution lessons. Why should a regional accent be important when she has a degree in science and communication policy from University College London, over ten years' experience as a financial journalist, is a highly skilled communicator, and was named Young Engineer of the Year? Why should this educated woman's voice be the thing that defines her in the opinion of some members of the public? There has also been media speculation about whether Prince Harry's voice played a role in attracting Meghan Markle, whether footballer David Beckham ever had elocution lessons to sound more authoritative as England captain, and some rather unkind comments about actor and presenter Donna Air losing her Geordie accent to sound a little posher to date Kate Middleton's brother. Clearly, how you speak still matters to a large number of people, or it simply would not be newsworthy.

In this book, I'll be mainly using the word 'voice' in the non-technical sense, i.e., as a cover term for the way that people produce speech and how that sounds. In technical terms—as far as phoneticians and speech therapists are concerned, for example—'voice' refers to how lung air causes there to be vibration or friction of various kinds at the vocal folds in the larynx (sometimes known as the voice box), creating sound for humans to modify into speech and language. This sound may have a variety of voice qualities, depending on things like how the speaker feels, what emotions or effects they want to convey, or whether there has been damage to the vocal folds.

For example, think about your own voice when you're tired. You can actually hear the tiredness in the voice.

There will be some reference to this meaning of the word 'voice' when we look at voice quality later in the book.

As a starting point, we're going to look at how a child's voice is influenced by the speech environment in the early years. To quote Maria from *The Sound of Music*, let's start at the very beginning.

Babies, children, and fish

It is usual to think that a child's first experience of people's voices happens when they are born into the world and start to hear language spoken around them. Actually, this is not the case. A child's linguistic journey starts much sooner than that. It starts while the child is still in the womb.

It is worth pausing here to briefly examine the physical phenomenon of sound. We perceive sound by way of our hearing apparatus consisting of the outer ear, the middle ear, and the inner ear. Sound itself comes to us from a source (for example, a person speaking, a musical instrument, the siren of an ambulance, the wind whistling down a chimney, the tinkling of a chandelier, the buzz of cicadas . . . the list is endless) and is carried through the air, moving away from the source in a series of waves which fan outwards.

Where speech is concerned, the speaker decides what it is they want to say, then the motor cortex in their brain sends signals to the muscles in the articulators, which include the lungs, the vocal folds (in the voice box or Adam's apple), the tongue, and the jaw. The lungs fill with air and the speaker starts to push the air out in a controlled way. The articulators move swiftly from position to position for various speech sounds, sometimes with the vocal folds producing voice, sometimes without, and these speech sounds are propelled via the pressure from the lungs into the air between the speaker and the listener.

Differences in air pressure due to the different kinds of sounds produced reach the ear of the listener. This causes the tympanic membrane, or eardrum, to vibrate, and three tiny bones (the ossicles) inside the inner ear transfer that vibration to liquid in the cochlea, or inner ear. The cochlea is shaped in a spiral, just like some seashells (for example, a conch shell or a whelk shell— you may have picked some up from the beach) and is filled with this liquid. Also inside the inner ear, spread along the entire length of the spiral, are tiny hairs, which vibrate according to the movement in the liquid caused by the movement of the three little bones. Electrical signals from the movement of these hairs then communicate to the brain what it is the listener has heard, and the brain finally makes sense of the message.

You can see a diagrammatical illustration of all of this in Figure 1.

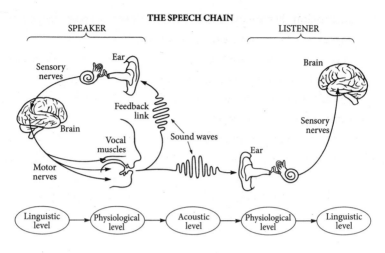

Figure 1 The speech chain

Air is important in transmission of sound from the source to your ear, as it acts as the carrier for sounds. There's a famous experiment with a ringing alarm clock inside a bell jar; when the air is pumped out of the bell jar, leaving a vacuum, it is no longer possible to hear the alarm clock ringing. As the tag line for the movie *Alien* observed, 'In space, no one can hear you scream'—that's because in space there is no air or other medium to carry sound.

 Scan here or go to https://www.youtube.com/watch?v=hlOqX4uJtYY to see Tan Aik Hwee's YouTube video of the bell jar experiment

You might think that, if a speaker's mouth and listener's ears were not surrounded by air, it would not be possible to hear sounds. However, other media can transmit sounds, although the effect you get is different from when air is the medium of transmission. Have you noticed when you're swimming that, to some extent, you can hear what's going on around you when you're underwater? And we get those hilarious cartoon-type high-pitched voices if you take in a mouthful of helium from a balloon[1]—but as soon as the helium disperses, we're back to boring old normal voice again.

Let's return to our unborn baby. A typically developing baby in the womb can hear the noises going on around their mother, even though the baby's ears are not surrounded by air. The baby can hear—and is listening to—all kinds of environmental sounds, the noises made by the mother's bodily functions . . . and speech.

All the parts of the inner ear described above are more or less in place by about the fifth month of a foetus's development. That means there is the possibility for sensitivity to sound from this point onwards. While we do not know exactly when an unborn child begins to attend to sound, what is clear from research carried out by Birgit Mampe, Kathleen Wermke, and colleagues[2] is that it is possible to identify which language group newly born babies (neonates) belong to based on the pitch patterns in their cries. The voice they will usually hear most loudly and clearly is their mother's and—while some of the sound is likely to come from the air around the mother—it will mainly be transmitted via the amniotic fluid around the foetus as the voice resonates through the mother's body. Try putting your fingers in your ears and count to five; you'll get an idea of what that might sound like.

The developing child will also be able to hear the voices of people their mother interacts with, the clearest signal being the falling and rising pitch of the voice. Again, if you think about how speech sounds underwater, we lose a lot of the fine detail but can still hear pitch differences. It's also a bit like when someone

7

has a loud party going on in the flat downstairs, when we might feel the sound more than hear it. Some people get quite excited around an expectant mother, and the physical manifestation of this includes increased pitch range; that is, their speech rises and falls in pitch in a much more exaggerated way. I've used capitals here for syllables which might have an exaggerated pitch: 'Oh my GOODness, you're PREGnant!' 'FanTASTic news!' 'When's it DUE?!' 'Is it KICKing? Can I FEEL??' etc. This is all being picked up and processed by the child's developing brain. I spent so much time around one of my friends when she was pregnant that, when the child was born, the only person other than his mother and father he would smile at for weeks following birth was me, and we think that's because he was already used to the sound of my voice and my pitch patterns.

The research showing that the cries of neonates have patterns of intonation similar to the language of their mother tongue is an indication that, as human beings, we are highly sensitive to speech. There are theories which claim we are cognitively pre-disposed to acquiring speech—in the 1960s, Noam Chomsky even suggested that we have a 'language acquisition device' in the brain (sometimes called the 'black box') which is only found in human beings. The existence of this 'black box' as a single, discrete area of the brain has not been proven; recent research using medical fMRI scans, for example, see that a number of areas across the brain are activated in speech and language acquisition and production. Researchers such as Sue Savage-Rumbaugh[3] and colleagues working with bonobo chimpanzees and other primates have also shown that it is possible for some non-human species to acquire and use language (but not speech) in a human-like way. What is certainly the case is that a newborn baby has physical, psychological, and social needs, and that nature has seen to it that she is able to have those needs satisfied by effectively causing her to fit in immediately with the social and linguistic group into which she arrives; her cries sound like the speech of people from the community. Language is important from the moment the child is born.

What happens in the first five years of a child's life is the development of an adult-like linguistic system based on the languages to which the child is exposed. In my case, I was only exposed to English, with my main influence in early childhood being parents who only spoke with a fairly standard Southeast England accent. It's actually more common in the world to be exposed to more than one language from birth. This happens, for example, if a child's parents or carers are bilingual or multilingual, or speak different varieties of the same language.

I'm going to give a short summary here of the acquisition of English speech sounds, as speech is the focus of the book, but there are many other aspects of language acquisition. If you're interested in that subject area, I suggest having a look at Jean Aitchison's excellent book *The articulate mammal*,[4] which was first published in 1976 and is so popular that it is now into its fifth edition.

In 1960, child language researchers Jean Berko and Roger Brown documented something now known as the 'fis phenomenon'.[5] What happened was that a child referred to his toy fish as a *fis*, but refused to accept *fis* as the correct production of *fish* from an adult. The exchange went something like this:

Adult: What's that you're playing with?
Child: A fis.

Adult: Is that your fis?
Child: No. My fis.

9

Adult: Your fis?

Child: No! My fis! My fis!

Adult: Is that your fish?

Child: Yes! My fis!

Berko and Brown used this example to show that the child could understand adult phonology, and the difference between certain speech sounds, before he could produce all the sounds himself. This means that linguistic categories are developing in the child's mind faster than he can articulate them; he knows there is a difference between the sounds at the end of *fis* (the phonetic symbol for it is [s]) and *fish* (phonetic symbol [ʃ]) but does not yet have enough control over the articulators in his mouth (mainly the tongue here) to make that difference. People have replicated this with their own children and posted videos on YouTube; search for 'fis phenomenon'.

We can tell that the child in Berko and Brown's study was probably at least three years of age, but he could be as old as seven. How do we know that?

In my work with speech and language therapy students, we have to consider what typically developing children do when they are acquiring their first language in order to work out whether a particular child has a problem—a speech and/or language deficit. One of the things we refer to is research on when children are able to produce certain kinds of speech sounds and use them correctly. Various studies have identified that there is an order of acquisition of consonant sounds in English, as there is in all languages. The order is shown in Figure 2, which indicates the age at which half of all typically developing children produce a consonant and use it correctly.

You can see that there is a lot of variation possible; a child might take up to five years to be able to produce, for

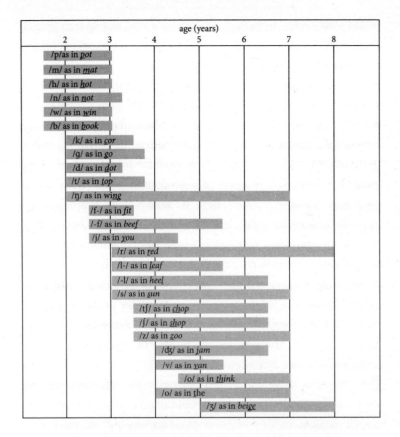

Figure 2 Age of acquisition of English speech sounds

example, /ŋ/ sounds (spelled *ng*) and /r/ sounds in an adult-like way, whereas the sounds /p t k b d g m n w/ and /h/ are usually acquired by the age of three-and-a-half. In the example from Berko and Brown, we can see that the child can produce /s/ but not /ʃ/, and so must be in a transitional stage between the ages of three and seven. We would need other data—including vocabulary scores and grammatical features—to be able to work out more precisely how old the child is.

Let's take some hypothetical data based on real speech from a child of 2.5 years, Nellie, interacting with her mother, Dawn. Dawn tries to get Nellie to say the word *fish*, and Nellie's production is variably something like /khap/, /jap/, and /hap/. This tallies well with the information in Figure 2. We would not expect Nellie to be able to produce the /f/ or /ʃ/ sounds in *fish* at the age of two-and-a-half, and indeed she does not produce them but uses other sounds fairly variably, with the exception of /p/ at the end of the word. But when Dawn repeats exactly what Nellie said back to her, Nellie rejects it until her mother correctly says the word *fish*. That's the 'fis phenomenon' at work. Babies and children are not just hearing language . . . they are listening and learning.

Although there are many differences in personality and how people's brains are wired, humans are basically social beings, and this also has an effect on language from an early age. As far as accent features are concerned, children's voices will usually sound very much like their caregivers' voices in the early years. Over time, as they come into contact with other people (for example, childminders and teachers) and get involved with different social groups (friendship groups, clubs and societies, even people from the television), the way they speak is likely to change. This change in the way people use their voices and adapt their accents according to different social situations continues throughout life for many. Do you have a 'telephone voice' when you have to call someone you don't know socially? Does your teenage son or daughter speak differently with you than they do with their best friend, or the parents of their best friend? If they do, this is normal, and the speakers themselves probably don't even realize it's happening (although I have friends who admit to having a telephone voice). Our voices evolve to show our social allegiances, our tribal memberships. This chameleon-like aspect of your voice is called code-switching or accommodation, and we are all speakers of many different codes.

Sounds, patterns, and codes

Understanding and producing language is all about being able to decipher and apply patterns and codes. Where speech sounds are concerned, our brains are basically biological computers performing huge feats of code-breaking every moment of every day. We need to be able to identify a given speech sound when a speaker produces it in the context of other speech sounds as part of a linguistic message. Not only do different people from the same accent group produce speech sounds slightly differently from others, every time we utter a speech sound, it is different. Amazingly, our brains are able to work it out. This can be more of a challenge when faced with an accent we don't understand but, given experience with that accent, our brain works it out.

So, what are the speech sounds of English?

There are many varieties of English (and many languages) in the world, so I'm going to stick to one British accent which is well documented as a reference from which to describe others. This accent is variously known as BBC English, General British (GB), Received Pronunciation (RP), or Southern British Standard (SBS), and is the variety usually found in dictionaries, reference books and British English language teaching materials.

This does not mean it is the 'correct' accent for English. It is one of many.

I'm going to follow Alan Cruttenden's terminology in the most recent edition of *Gimson's pronunciation of English*[6] and use General British in the sections which follow.

Consonants

GB is usually described as having forty-four individual phonemes (for the purposes of this description, a phoneme is a speech sound in a given language, but there will be some more discussion of this term later on). Of these forty-four sounds, twenty are vowel sounds and twenty-four are consonants. The *Cambridge English pronouncing dictionary*[7] gives the following keywords for GB consonants, with all but one (*hang*) referring to the first consonant sound in the word:

Voiceless	Voiced
p as in *pea*	b as in *bee*
t as in *tea*	d as in *do*
k as in *key*	g as in *go*
f as in *fat*	v as in *vat*
θ as in *thin*	ð as in *that*
s as in *sip*	ʃ as in *ship*
h as in *hat*	
	m as in *map*
	n as in *nap*
	ŋ as in *hang*
	l as in *led*
	r as in *red*
	j as in *yet*
	w as in *wet*
tʃ as in *chin*	dʒ as in *gin*

You'll have noticed these are organized with some on the left and some on the right. The symbols on the left represent consonant sounds produced without vibration of the vocal folds ('voiceless' consonants), and the ones on the right are produced with vibration of the vocal folds ('voiced' consonants).

To test this, put your hand on your throat where your voice box is, and say the sound /s/ as long as possible: 'sssssssssssss'. You shouldn't feel any vibration in the larynx when you say this sound.

Now change to /z/: 'zzzzzzzzzzzzzz'. You should be able to feel vibration when you say this sound. (I love doing this with my students and seeing their reactions.)

This technique works well for all consonant sounds except the six at the top of the list, voiceless /p t k/ and voiced /b d g/, and the two at the bottom, voiceless /tʃ/ and voiced /dʒ/. This is because of the type of sounds they are. With the other sounds, as long as you have air in your lungs, you can keep producing them. But these eight sounds involve stopping the air and then releasing it in a burst.

Let's try saying the sound /p/ as an example. If you put your hand in front of your mouth and say 'aapaa', you should be able to feel the warmth of your breath for the first 'aa', then everything stopping as you close your lips to say the /p/, and then a burst of air as you open your lips and resume the 'aa'. These sounds are called 'plosive' consonants because there is an explosion of air as you say them. We get the explosion because the air is held in the mouth and can't go anywhere else, causing air pressure to build up until the closure (in this case, the upper and lower lip pressed together tightly) is opened.

Because you have to stop the air to say them, it's very difficult to compare the sounds /p/ and /b/ in the same way as, for example, /s/ and /z/. So, how can you compare them and tell them apart? By comparing the strength of the burst of air.

If you put your hand in front of your mouth and say 'aapaa' and 'aabaa', you should be able to feel that the /p/ sound has a stronger burst than the /b/ sound. This difference is in something known as aspiration; in GB, we say that /p/ is aspirated (has a strong burst of air after it) and /b/ is not aspirated. However, accents of English differ in this respect, so you may not have the same pattern. I demonstrated this phenomenon on the Alan Titchmarsh television show, and we discovered that Alan's accent might have different patterns of aspiration.[8]

/tʃ/ and /dʒ/ in *chain* and *Jane* are not plosives but affricates. An affricate is a sound which begins by stopping the air, like a plosive, but—instead of releasing the air relatively quickly and cleanly—the air is released in the manner of a fricative sound. Compare *tip* and *chip* which start with /t/ and /tʃ/ respectively.

Which sounds are fricatives in English? /f θ s ʃ h/ (voiceless) and /v ð z ʒ/ (voiced).

I've explained how plosives are produced. How about fricatives?

Fricatives are like plosive sounds in that they are produced under pressure. A small gap is made in the articulators and the air is forced through the gap. This results in a hissing sound. The hissing is most obvious with /f θ s ʃ/. Try producing each one of those on their own and observe the hissing noise.

Plosives, fricatives, and affricates all involve an obstruction to the air, in which the air is under pressure in the mouth, or oral cavity. In order to achieve this pressure, one other vital component is needed: the air must not be allowed to pass through the nose. This means the soft palate must be raised to block the air off. I think it's time to have a look at the articulators.

The picture in Figure 3 is a diagram of the side of the head, as if someone had sliced from top to bottom. It is labelled with terms describing parts of the oral cavity (inside of the mouth) involved in the articulation of speech. What we can't see clearly here are

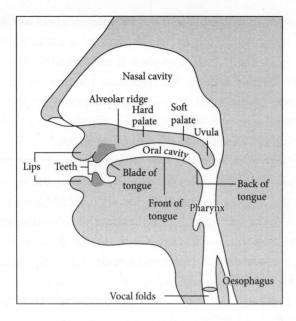

Figure 3   The organs of speech

the sides of the tongue, or the teeth, which go all the way around on both sides of the oral cavity.

Let's take a journey through the articulators. Start by pressing your lips together. In the articulation of speech sounds, we talk about active and passive articulators, with the active articulator moving towards and/or coming into contact with the passive articulator. It's usual to think of the parts labelled across the top of this diagram as passive, as they can't move, and the lower lip and tongue to as active, as they are more mobile and move around easily. We can, of course, move our top lip quite a lot (try it!), but it is fixed to the upper mandible (just above your top teeth and below your nose), which doesn't move. Your lower lip is attached to the lower mandible, which is part of the jaw and highly mobile. You can press your lips together without moving the jaw very much, but if you open the jaw your bottom lip will move away from the top lip. Sounds made using both lips pressed together are called 'bilabial' sounds (literally, 'two lips'), and in English these are /p/, /b/, and /m/.

Another sound we make using the lips is /w/, which involves rounding the lips and pushing them out slightly. We'll come back to /w/ later as there's more going on than just lip movement.

We can also make sounds with the bottom lip against the upper teeth. These sounds are 'labiodental', and in English are /f/ and /v/. Try making these sounds.

Now I want you to run your tongue tip slowly from the cutting edge of your teeth back towards the velum, also known as the soft palate. As you run it backwards, you can feel: 1) the backs of the teeth; 2) a bony ridge, followed by 3), a sudden upwards curve; 4) the curve of the roof of your mouth, first bony, then 5) soft. We make dental sounds /θ/ and /ð/ between the back of the teeth and the tongue tip. The bony ridge is called the alveolar ridge, and sounds produced there are alveolar consonants /t/, /d/, /s/, /z/, /n/, and /l/. Say the words *tip*, *dip*, *sip*, *zip*, *nip*, and *lip*, which begin with these consonants, to try them. Some types of /r/ sound are also made there. Can you roll your /r/ sounds using your tongue tip, like in Spanish? That's made on the alveolar ridge. My primary school singing teacher always got us lot in the choir to roll our *r* sounds. The technical term for this is 'trilling'.

Sounds /ʃ/, /ʒ/, /tʃ/, /dʒ/, and what's thought of as the 'normal' General American /r/ sound are made with the tongue behind the alveolar ridge, at the sudden curve upwards—number 3) above. For each of these sounds, say the words *shoe*, *jus* ('zhoo'—the French word used in cooking—OK, I know it's a bit pretentious, but /ʒ/ is a pretty infrequent sound in English!), *chew*, *Jew*, and *rue*, which all rhyme, and focus on the initial consonant sound. If you compare *sip* with *ship*, you should be able to feel the difference in tongue position between alveolar sounds (/s/ is alveolar) and these ones, which are called post-alveolar (that is, just after the alveolar ridge).

The next sound to try is /j/ at the start of *yet*, which is palatal. Don't confuse it with the letter *j*, which is usually produced as the affricate /dʒ/ as in *Jane*. When you make the /j/ sound, the tongue bunches up and approaches the hard palate but doesn't actually touch it (but you should be able to feel the sides of the tongue against the teeth). This type of sound is called an approximant, and involves bending the air around rather than stopping it or forcing it through a narrow gap. Another type of approximant is a lateral approximant, and in English the only one is alveolar /l/. We call this lateral as we make tongue-tip contact on the bony ridge behind the teeth, but the sides of the tongue are low. If you make the shape for /l/ and breathe in, you should be able to feel the cold air flow along the sides of your tongue.

The last approximant sound to try is /w/. We already met this sound when we were looking at lip movement, but there's more to /w/ than meets the eye—quite literally. We can see the lips rounding when someone produces /w/, but something else is going on; the back of the tongue moves up towards the soft palate at the same time as the lips are rounded, and this is not visible from outside. Try saying 'aawaa' and focus on what is happening with your tongue. You should feel the back bunches up a bit and moves upwards. We call /w/ 'labial-velar' as it has two places of articulation: the lips round, and the back of the tongue moves towards the soft palate.

Other sounds involving the back of the tongue and the soft palate are /k/ in *core*, /g/ in *gore*, and /ŋ/ at the end of *song*. /k/ and /g/ are both types of plosive, completely blocking the air, and

/ŋ/ is a nasal consonant. Try saying them and feel where your tongue is as you do.

/m/, /n/, and /ŋ/ are all nasal consonants. If you've got a cold, you may not be able to produce these sounds or breathe in on them. That's because, when we make these sounds, the air escapes through the nose. If your nose is blocked, an /m/ will sound like a /b/, a /n/ like a /d/, and a /ŋ/ like a /g/. We'll see in Chapter 4 how one particular type of voice uses that to advantage.

Nasal consonants are exactly the same as plosives, except that the soft palate is lowered so that air pressure does not build up in the oral cavity but passes out through the nose. In the case of /b/ and /m/, for example, the soft palate is raised for /b/—as we don't want the air to be able to escape until we open the lips—but lowered for /m/ so the air can pass out through the nose. When we produce /b/, there is air pressure build-up, but not for /m/.

You can feel this physically by trying to say this sequence of sounds without opening your lips: /bmbmbmbmbmbm/.

Can you feel the differences in air pressure?

You may also be able to feel your soft palate lowering in the upper back region of your mouth as you do this. We don't usually think about what the soft palate is doing and so don't generally notice it.

Another way we can tell the air is coming through the nasal cavity is to place the glass of your mobile phone or a small mirror under your nose and then produce two sounds, one without nasal airflow and one with.

First, say a long, sustained /s/.

/sssssssssssss/

What can you see on the mirror / your phone? (Tip: there shouldn't be anything there as /s/ does not have nasal airflow.)

Now try a long /n/.

/nnnnnnnnnnn/

You should be able to see water vapour on the glass from the air coming up from your lungs and through the nasal cavity.

One consonant which is not on this list but is very common in English accents is called a 'glottal stop' or 'glottal plosive', and it's made by pressing the vocal folds tightly together. The symbol for this sound is [ʔ] . . . and you may notice it's in a different set of brackets from the others. There's a reason for that.

First, try making this sound. You can do this by coughing very gently. When you do this, you close the vocal folds, hold them shut for a short while, then release them to produce the burst of air we associate with all plosive consonants. We cough because we are trying to remove an irritant in the throat, and the only way the body has of doing this is using highly pressurized air. The best way of producing air pressure build-up in that area is to close the vocal folds and push air out of the lungs.

Now try producing this sound as a speech sound. You may have it in your accent anyway. Say the word *hotter*, and try doing the gentle cough instead of the /t/ sound. If you do this, both the spoken consonants in this word in the GB accent are glottal— that's the /h/ and the [ʔ].

The glottal stop gets a bit of a bad press. It's particularly associated with London accents spoken by people from less educated backgrounds. When speakers use it to replace /t/, they are often described as speaking in a slovenly manner. But actually, it's used by speakers from many backgrounds, and is not out of place in the reference accent, GB. The main difference is that accents considered to be less prestigious use it in words like *hotter* where it is between two vowel sounds. In more prestigious accents, it tends to get used more often at the ends of words and not between vowels, and is therefore less obvious.

Take the phrase 'isn't it?' Where a speaker of old-fashioned RP would most likely pronounce both /t/ sounds, a modern speaker of GB is more likely to have a glottal stop at the end of *it*.

But why have I put it in square brackets, [ʔ]? This is because, in English, it always stands in for another plosive consonant— usually /t/. When a speaker uses it and a listener hears it, they understand /t/. If I substitute [ʔ] for /t/ in a word like *hotter*, it makes no difference in meaning. [ʔ] is therefore a production variant of /t/. We call this an allophone.

However, if I substitute any of the other sounds for /t/, potentially I can change the meaning of the word. All of the words *sat, sad, sam, sang, sap, sack, sag* start with the same two sounds, but the final consonant is different in each case, and they all mean different things. This shows that /t d m ŋ p k/ and /g/ are all different meaning units in English: they are phonemes. If I have [ʔ] at the end, however, listeners will perceive *sat*. It doesn't mean anything different from /t/.

To use a phrase from *The Matrix*, this might be baking your noodle right now. Let's move on to vowels.

Vowels

Vowels have got to be less complex, right? After all, English only has five of them: A, E, I, O, and U ... doesn't it?

Nope.

The General British accent actually has twenty vowel phonemes, and a couple of others thrown in for good measure. It's complex. Anyone working with children who are learning to spell will realize this is not a straightforward area.

For vowels, I will use the keywords from John Wells's Standard Lexical Sets.[9] One of the reasons for doing this is because almost all work describing accents of English since the publication of the Standard Lexical Sets in the 1980s uses the Wells framework to talk about vowel variation.

The words to represent each vowel sound given in CAPITALS below were chosen because they cannot easily be confused with other words. The remaining words in each line are examples of how the vowel appears in English spelling.

1. KIT ship, kid, limp, myth, build...
2. DRESS step, ebb, tent, bread, friend...
3. TRAP tap, rag, hand, lapse, plaid...
4. LOT stop, odd, box, swan, wash...
5. STRUT cup, bud, lump, come, touch...
6. FOOT put, bush, good, wolf, could...
7. BATH staff, class, ask, fasten, laugh...
8. CLOTH off, cross, soft, cough, Austin...
9. NURSE hurt, birth, church, verb, word...
10. FLEECE creep, need, cheese, brief, field...
11. FACE tape, fade, waist, play, reign...
12. PALM calm, ma, hurrah, façade, Java...
13. THOUGHT cause, taunt, hawk, chalk, broad...
14. GOAT soap, joke, host, toe, mauve...
15. GOOSE loop, mood, tomb, two, fruit...
16. PRICE ripe, side, child, try, eye...
17. CHOICE boy, noise, spoil, employ, hoist...
18. MOUTH out, crowd, cow, round, bough...
19. NEAR beer, here, pier, fear, pierce...
20. SQUARE share, fair, bear, where, scarce...
21. START far, sharp, carve, heart, safari...

22. NORTH for, orb, form, quart, cord...
23. FORCE fore, soar, floor, court, sword...
24. CURE moor, your, sure, gourd, fury...
25. happY copy, khaki, movie, coffee, money...
26. lettER paper, sugar, standard, anchor, martyr...
27. commA quota, visa, panda, sofa, saga...
28. thankYOU evaluate...

As you're reading through these words, you might be thinking to yourself, 'Hang on—I've got the same vowel sound in TRAP and BATH', or 'The way I say NORTH is no different from how I say THOUGHT or FORCE' (or even CURE). That's the clever bit about this list. John Wells noticed that there are groups of words which some people say differently and some do not, and it is from these observations that this list arose. The differences are mainly down to the historical development of English accents over time in different areas of the British Isles, in other countries where English is spoken, and also owing to differences in social status. Most people from the North of England and from the United States, for example, have the same vowel in TRAP and BATH, but for the majority of speakers from the South of England the vowels will be different. What should not be the case is that you say words in each set differently; for example, all words in the START set should have the same vowel, whether or not START has the same vowel as BATH.

Here are the words in the lexical sets organized according to the vowel sounds they have in General British, together with the vowel symbols used in this book; these are the ones you see in most British English pronunciation text books. Both northern and southern standard variants are indicated, where relevant.

'Short' vowel monophthongs (six of these)
KIT /ɪ/
DRESS /e/
TRAP /æ/
LOT, CLOTH /ɒ/
STRUT south /ʌ/, north /ʊ/
FOOT /ʊ/

'Long' vowel monophthongs (five of these)
BATH south /ɑ:/, north /æ/ (short in northern accents);
    PALM, START /ɑ:/
NURSE /ɜ:/
FLEECE /i:/
THOUGHT, NORTH, FORCE /ɔ:/
GOOSE /u:/

'Long' vowel diphthongs (eight of these)
GOAT /əʊ/
MOUTH /aʊ/
FACE /eɪ/
PRICE /aɪ/
CHOICE /ɔɪ/
NEAR /ɪə/
SQUARE /eə/—sometimes transcribed /ɛ:/
CURE /ʊə/

Weak vowels (three of these)
lettER, commA /ə/
happy /i/
thank yOU /u/

Let's look a bit more at the set described as 'weak vowels'.

Traditionally, the vowel at the end of lettER and commA, known as 'schwa' and symbolized /ə/, is included in the twenty vowels of General British...but the happY and thank yOU vowels are not. This is because, among speakers with older versions of RP, the happY and thankyOU vowels would have been pronounced /ɪ/ as in KIT (for happY) and /ʊ/ as in FOOT (for thankyOU). Speakers of General British tend to pronounce the vowel at the end of happY as more of a cross between the FLEECE vowel and the KIT vowel, and the one in thank yOU as a cross between the GOOSE and the FOOT vowel. The important thing to note is that we are only talking about these vowels in certain positions, which is that they are never stressed.

Something else you may have noticed is that vowels are described as monophthongs and diphthongs. What's the difference between a monophthong and a diphthong?

When we produce vowel sounds, the vowel we get depends on where our tongue is positioned in the mouth. The vowel in START (in British English) is very like the one doctors ask you to say when they want to look at the back of your throat—'Say "aaaahhhh", please!' (depresses tongue with flat implement). Try saying 'aaaahhhh' now. Your tongue stays in one place when you say this vowel, and so we describe it as a monophthong ('mono' = one; 'phthong' = sound).

If you say the vowel in PRICE, however, your tongue starts in one place and moves to another. It goes on a little journey. We can see and feel this better with the word *eye*, which contains only that vowel with no consonant sounds. Try it. Can you feel your tongue and jaw closing as you produce this vowel? As there are two tongue positions involved, we call it a diphthong ('di' = two; 'phthong' = sound).

The terms 'long' and 'short' are also used in the list. The difference between long and short vowels depends on context and position in a word. The position part can be dealt with the most easily: there are no single syllable content[10] words in GB containing a short vowel which do not end with at least one consonant, either in spelling or in pronunciation. Examples include *cat*, *sing*, *shot*, *hut*, and *fed*. Single- syllable words containing long vowel monophthongs and diphthongs, by comparison, do not have to have consonant sounds after them, but they can do. Examples without consonant sounds include *play*, *lie*, *boy*, *see*, and *saw*.

When the Ford motor company decided to name its smallest car the KA, this drove me nuts. Why? Because of the rule above, people felt compelled to pronounce KA as *car* (/kɑː/), containing the START vowel, as it cannot be a short vowel. But to me—from both a spelling and pronunciation point of view—it was /kæ/, with a TRAP vowel . . . which is illegal in GB. I'm told by people in car sales that it's supposed to be pronounced /keɪ eɪ/ ('kay-eh'), but I've never heard anyone call it that. Have you read about those people who wander round with a marker pen correcting bad grammar on signs? I think Lynne Truss says something about this in her book *Eat, shoots and leaves*.[11] I've managed to stop myself adding the letter *r* to the logo on Ford KAs, but it makes me cringe every time I pass one. If it's supposed to be pronounced 'kay-ey', it should be K.A., surely?

Stress and intonation

When I was talking about babies earlier in this chapter, I mentioned that the pitch of the voice rises and falls as people speak, and that this is increased when they are excited about something—that is, when they are emotionally involved.

Intonation is sometimes described as 'the melody of speech'. It is very unusual in human languages for speech to be produced without melodies, or to be monotone (like the speech of the Daleks in *Doctor Who*—but even these sometimes have a rise in pitch at the end). As with all linguistic features of speech, these melodies have patterns which are specific to particular languages.

In some languages—like Chinese dialects and indigenous languages spoken in Africa and South America—changes of pitch on a single syllable can change the meaning of the word. These are called tone languages. A commonly given example is how tones change the meaning of the syllable *ma* in Mandarin Chinese. Mandarin Chinese has four tones and, depending on which tone you use, this syllable can mean 'mother', 'horse', 'hemp', and 'to scold'. (You can easily find examples of this if you do an online search.)

English does not operate in the same way, but we do have some interesting patterns of word stress and intonation which can change the meaning of a word or an utterance.

There are several words which change from nouns or adjectives to verbs if the stress is different. For example, if the word *record* is a noun (meaning item on or in which information is stored), we stress the first syllable—i.e., the first syllable is louder and longer than the second syllable and the pitch is slightly higher: *RECord*. If it's a verb (meaning to create that item on or in which information is stored), the stress is on the second syllable: *reCORD*.

Think about the word *perfect*: what does it mean if you pronounce it *PERfect* in comparison with *perFECT*? ('That's the perfect gift for her,' versus 'I'm going to perfect my icing technique.')

Intonation is speaker-specific as well as language specific. What I mean by this is that everyone has their own average spoken pitch and pitch range. We measure spoken pitch in Hertz, which is basically the number of vibrations per second of the vocal folds during voicing. If you growl in your throat, you may be able to hear individual vibrations of the vocal folds (this can be used in speech and is referred to as 'creak' or 'vocal fry'—more on this in Chapter 3). In normal speech, the vocal folds usually vibrate much more quickly than this. Among men, average pitch is around 100–150 cycles (vocal fold vibrations) per second. Among women, it is usually double that, and among children it is three to four times more. Average pitch usually drops as people age—very noticeably so for men, whose voice 'breaks' during puberty and suddenly becomes much lower in pitch.

In languages, many features of intonation are similar. For example, if you ask a question, your pitch often goes up at the end (but not always!) and, in statements, it often goes down. This is common across many languages. However, as we'll see in the chapters which follow, this is not always the case, and there are some interesting patterns of pitch and intonation use which can signal which social group an individual belongs to, as well as indicating linguistic meaning.

Patterns and codes

Every language has its own set of distinctive sounds, and these sounds operate in patterns, such as the rules in the GB accent where the glottal stop can only stand in for /t/ when it is not between vowel sounds, or /ŋ/ only occurring at the ends of words. In Cantonese, for example, /ŋ/ can occur at the begin-nings of words—the word for *I* in Cantonese is /ŋo/, spoken with a rising tone. As speakers of particular languages, these rules form during childhood and can be hard to shift in adulthood, which is one reason why it is more difficult for us to learn languages later in life, and particularly difficult for language learners to have native-like accents.

This is also the case for the patterns in different accents of a language. Just because someone speaks a given language (e.g. English), it doesn't mean their accent will be easily understood by other speakers of that language, as the patterns can be very different. We'll look more at this in Chapter 2, where we look at British English accents and accent prejudice.

What is certain, however, is that languages are rule-based and have identifiable, regular patterns. If they were random, we wouldn't be able to understand each other. We rely on patterns in order to be able to decode the message we are listening to. Every speaker has slightly different patterns, but they correspond generally to the overall pattern of a particular accent. This is why, when you hear someone you haven't met before from the same accent group as you speak for the first time, it can take a couple of seconds to understand them, but our brain is really good at accommodating to new voices if the accent is one you are familiar with. It's also one of the reasons we have predictable social greetings like 'Nice to meet you', as it gives the brain time off from understanding the message so it can calibrate itself to the speaker's voice and accent. If someone says something less predictable, it can throw the brain off. And if someone has a less familiar accent, it can take a lot longer to get used to the patterns.

Here's an example from when I was a child. I had a school friend whose parents were from Scotland, and her father was from Glasgow. When I met him, the first thing he said wasn't something predictable like 'Hello' or 'Nice to meet you', which are quite common as greetings. Oh no. It was 'Will you no have a chair?'

And I didn't understand him.

Not just because the grammar was unusual to me, or because it was an unexpected greeting, but also because his accent and pronunciation were very different from anything I had ever heard.

My friend's mother—whom I'd met before and whose accent was not so broad—then said, 'Won't you sit down?' It was only at that point that her father's words suddenly made sense. My brain needed time (and a translation) to work it out.

After that, I had less difficulty understanding my friend's father, as I'd got used to his voice... but it did take me a bit longer to get used to his accent.

What's coming up?

Here's an overview of the rest of this book.

In Chapter 2, I'll be looking at accents of the UK. The focus here is on how speakers of different accents are perceived, but there will also be an overview of how we came to have all these accents in the first place. You may be surprised to learn just how hybrid and 'foreign' the English language is.

There are lots of myths about speech and language, and Chapter 3 covers those specific to speech. Can men make their voices sound sexy? Do only young people have the kind of intonation which goes up at the end? Are women's voices 'worse' than men's voices? And so on.

Had you noticed how some singers have one accent when they sing, and another when they speak? Chapter 4 investigates this phenomenon, and also looks at other language professionals and whether they change the way they speak in their professional environment.

Can speech be used to catch criminals? In my role as a forensic phonetician, I have worked on a number of cases comparing the speech from, for example, telephone recordings with police interviews. Chapter 5 explains how this works, and also considers the field of speaker profiling, in which phoneticians try to identify a person's origins from a speech sample.

Chapter 6 is on people whose voices have been changed in some way other than accent features to reflect their identity. There are examples from transgender speakers, and machines which produce speech for people who are unable to do so themselves.

Finally, Chapter 7 rounds off the discussion by looking briefly at speakers of English around the world, including some observations on speech and ethnicity. There is then an annotated bibliography (list of books and papers) for anyone wishing to delve into the subject of voice in any greater detail.

I hope you enjoy the book, and find this subject as fascinating as I do. If you'd like to chat with me about it, or even take me to task, you can find me on Twitter: @JaneSetter.

CHAPTER 2

The Watling Street divide
Romans, Anglo-Saxons, Vikings, and accent prejudice

An Englishman's way of speaking absolutely classifies him; the moment he talks, he makes another Englishman despise him.

Henry Higgins, *My Fair Lady*

H ere's a hypothetical situation based on a real case.

Alison Davies is an actor who grew up in Liverpool. As a young teenager, she appeared in an extremely popular children's television programme based in an area of the city, and became a household name as one of the cast. She released a single with a couple of the other actors after a few years on the show, and toured the world as a pop star for a short time. There were television and radio interviews talking about the popularity of the show and what it was like to make the move into the pop scene.

During this period, Alison had an identifiable, but not very strong, Scouse (Liverpool) accent, like most of the young actors in the programme. That was one of the selling points of the show. Some of the actors had much broader accents and some had more standard-sounding accents.

Alison's pop career didn't last, but she went on to become a successful broadcaster and actor. She was still a household name in her early thirties.

Suddenly, the media started to pick up on the way Alison spoke. People started noticing that her accent had changed quite a bit. She had gone from quite obviously Scouse to something nearer RP. That is, she sounded more 'posh'. Questions were asked in the press and on television chat shows. Gossip was rife. Had her accent changed because she had been dating someone with a British public school education? Was she shunning her Liverpool roots in order to fit in with her new social group, and was her speech an indication of that?

Some commentators made particularly unkind remarks, ridiculing the way she spoke and accusing her of ambitious social climbing. An afternoon chat show asked its guests to listen to her and mimic the way she spoke, eliciting gales of laughter from the studio audience. Alison Davies had become a laughing stock because of the way she spoke.

A national newspaper then noticed that Alison seemed to be 'going back to her Scouse roots', meaning aspects of her regional accent were reasserting themselves. As far as the newspaper was concerned, this was a subject worthy of coverage—something people needed to know about. Why should she have changed back to Scouse? Was she trying to look friendlier and less aloof? Was she trying to reconnect with her local origins and fans? Accent experts (including me) were called in to comment.

In Britain—and elsewhere in the world—we suffer hugely from accent prejudice, or 'accentism'. Accent prejudice is part of a larger phenomenon known as 'linguicism'—basically, being prejudiced against someone for his or her use of language. Where accent prejudice is concerned, people are quick to comment in a scathing way not only about accents but also when someone changes the way they speak. But the truth is we can't always pinpoint why people do or do not change the way they speak—and they might not be able to pinpoint it themselves... or even know they are doing it.

There are people who are social chameleons, slipping easily from one accent or spoken style to another, sometimes consciously, sometimes not.

There are others who, for one reason or another, steadfastly hold on to one accent throughout their lives. An example of this is a British colleague of mine who spent almost his entire working life in the United States. He never picked up a trace of an American accent. Another British colleague working in the States made such a conscious effort not to pick up an American accent that, when she came back to the UK to visit, her family and friends said she sounded Australian!

One of my reasons for writing this book is that I've noticed accentism going on around me. I've even been the subject of it. So, what's my experience of accent prejudice, other than being asked to comment on the speech of others for the national press?

Growing up as a child at primary school in the 1970s, other kids always used to tease me about being posh—and they could be really quite nasty about it, just like the unkind comments on Alison's accent.

At the time, I never really understood why they teased me. We lived in a small terraced house, like most of my primary school mates, who either lived—as did my family—in the Victorian terrace-lined streets near the school, or in council housing on the other side of the main road. My parents had working-class backgrounds, and were not highly paid professionals, both holding down two part-time jobs to make ends meet. We hardly ever went on overseas holidays, had a new car, or bought much in the way of modern conveniences. There was great excitement on the day my dad brought home a cassette recorder so we could play Abba and Tammy Wynette tapes in the car (and I could sing along loudly—more on this later). But the neighbourhood kids weren't really interested in being friends with me, and some of their parents were rather stand-offish. I got on best with two other outcasts, both of whose families were from overseas. I found their home environments fascinating capsules of different cultures, and their parents very welcoming.

It wasn't until much later that I realized this judgement of me and of my parents was partly because of the way we spoke—I was being ostracized because my accent was different. I was a victim of accentism.

It wasn't really my fault I spoke the way I did; like I said in Chapter 1, any sign of regional variation in my speech, and my dad's disapproval would come down on me like a ton of bricks. My friends, whose families were from Scandinavia and Hong Kong, also spoke much closer to Southern British Standard than the other kids, and their families had foreign accents, so they were socially very different.

We have a lot of variety in regional accents in Britain, and the way you speak is still very much a marker of regional and social background. It can denote where we come from, and it's sometimes possible to locate people to very precise regions of the country. In that respect, it is tribal.

It can also denote something many like to think doesn't (or shouldn't) exist any more in Britain: class. But class is so ingrained in the British psyche that it's just too difficult to dislodge. The fact that we have a monarchy may well be something to do with it. Our figurehead epitomizes British upper-class speech: 'The Queen's English'.

But how did we get to this state of affairs—particularly in England—and how does it affect the way people are viewed in today's society? Let me take you on a short historical journey through the very early origins of accents of English in (mainly) England, and then we'll review some of the research around accents and how they are perceived.

Early beginnings

All languages are organic. Human language evolved over thousands of years and experienced many changes and developments to enable us to express complex ideas. There is no language that can be considered 'pure'. There are some very old languages (for example, Sanskrit), but they are all a mixture of influences. Modern languages are evolving all the time. Language change is here to stay, and it is as inevitable as it is fascinating. As the French say, 'Plus ça change, plus c'est la même chose'—the more things change, the more they stay the same.

I'm just going to pause to note there that the word for 'change' is the same in English and French. Interesting, eh? Where do you think the English language got that word from? French certainly didn't borrow the word in from English.

English is a hybrid language, and is not the indigenous language of the British Isles. The language we speak today is basically Germanic, with a good dollop of French, and a measure of Latin. This is the result of invasion and the historical influence of powerful social groups, such as the Church and the State.

37

You've probably heard of the Viking invasions of the British Isles and of the Norman Conquest of 1066. What you may not realize is that, without these invasions and other linguistic interventions, the English speakers in England would likely all be speaking something closer to Welsh—we'd be Celtic language speakers.

You may also know that Britain was invaded by the Romans before the Vikings and Normans. The Romans were in Britain between 43 and 410 AD, but didn't get much further up the country than Hadrian's Wall. Yes, the Picts and the Scots held them off!

What's interesting is that the Romans seem to have left little trace on the language we now speak, even though they were around for almost 400 years.

The languages spoken in Britain at the time of the Roman invasion of 43 AD are known as Insular Celtic languages. The speakers of these languages were themselves migrants, coming to Britain and Ireland as early as the Bronze Age (around 2100–750 BC), before the Romans arrived from continental Europe. They are usually thought to have integrated peacefully with earlier people, who also migrated from Europe and whose descendants built the various henges and barrows around the country, such as Stonehenge and West Kennett Longbarrow in Wiltshire. DNA analysis carried out recently on the fossil remains of 'Cheddar Man' show that these earlier people had dark or black skin and hair, and blue eyes.[1] Skin colour changed over time, probably to allow Britons to absorb more sunlight, hence increasing natural production of Vitamin D.

It is likely that the Insular Celts came because of the natural resources Britain had, like copper and tin, and the rich farming lands. It is unclear how much Insular Celtic languages were mutually intelligible, however, and they split sometime before the Dark Ages into two main groups: Gaelic in Ireland, and

Brittonic in England and some parts of Scotland. British Latin also developed to communicate with the Romans, and it is likely that Latin was used in Christian worship, introduced by the Romans to England, Wales, and southern parts of Scotland.

This lack of mutual intelligibility among speakers of Insular Celtic varieties in different regions of Britain is not really surprising given that, by the end of the Bronze age, there were probably no more than 100,000 people spread throughout the island—that's not too dissimilar to the current population of Basingstoke in Hampshire—and communities tended to stay put and not move around much. Linguistic development depends on a number of things, one being whether people are coming into contact with others and needing— or wanting—to communicate with them. If they are not, any linguistic development will be very much based on local needs without reference to what's going on elsewhere. This leads to mutually unintelligible varieties of a language. It's still happening now, with the development of varieties of English around the world.

If you wanted to get from A to B during the Dark Ages, you either had to walk or use a cart pulled by a horse, donkey, or other beast of burden. It takes me around thirty-five minutes to get to work in my car, but it would take nearly four hours to walk the same distance. A four-hour walk to reach a more densely populated area might be worth it if, say, I had to travel to market from a rural area to sell produce in order to make a living, but it's unlikely that a journey of that kind would happen daily. Towns and cities in Britain to this day have a weekly 'market day', and you'd often find settlements in proximity to each other would have their market days on consecutive days of the week to maximize the chance of someone selling their produce without having to travel too far every day to do it.

Also, it would probably be just one or two from a community doing the travelling. People were needed at home to feed livestock, tend crops, and look after children, and you wouldn't want to leave your home unattended in case of raids. This meant less chance for people from different villages to come into contact with each other ... and a greater chance of accent features and dialect words forming in that community which were not used by outsiders.

What the Romans did for us: the Anglo-Saxons

OK, so we have a picture of what Britain looked like linguistically before and during the Roman occupation. But the regional differences we have in UK accents now were largely put in place after the Romans left. The Romans, however, were partly responsible for those regional differences.

Historic texts mainly written after the Romans left Britain explain that large groups of people from other parts of the Roman Empire—notably the areas now known as northern Germany and Denmark, but also some from northern France—came to Britain either to work for the Romans (building those famous Roman roads, for example) or by the request of the Britons, to help defend them from other tribes such as the Picts and the Scots. Those invited by treaty to help defend the Britons were given lands in the east of England in return—places like East Anglia, Cambridgeshire, and the Humberside area. The bulk of the migration seems to have taken place from the fifth century AD onwards and, while some early historical accounts suggested that these people came as invaders, more recent archaeology suggests that they settled peacefully. While they were not a homogeneous group, they were later grouped together and called the Anglo-Saxons. They brought their language with them, a language which is now known as Old English. The word *English* itself derives from 'Angle-ish'.

But Old English was not a homogeneous language, with different varieties depending on the origin of the speakers who brought it. Much like the Insular Celts, they would have lived in settlements quite distant from each other, as people feel most comfortable in their own social groups and are suspicious of outsiders. There were also a large number of 'kings', or tribal leaders, at this time, each one commanding loyalty. The variety of a language you speak is a strong marker of whether or not you belong to a particular social group or community.

What's particularly interesting is what happened to the languages of the Britons. They spoke either Celtic and/or British Latin at the time the Anglo-Saxons arrived. Unless they were associated with the Christian Church and needed Latin for that, they eventually abandoned those languages and all ended up speaking one or other variety of Old English. Why should this be the case? Why choose the language of the invaders?

Various scenarios are possible, including a theory that the Anglo-Saxons were so scary and vicious that they either killed or frightened away the people who spoke other languages—but this now seems uncertain. Regions with a greater concentration of Celtic language speakers were in and near the region we now know as Wales—in fact, the word *Welsh* itself derives from the Germanic word for 'foreign', because Celts were foreigners as far as the Anglo-Saxons were concerned—and in the Southwest. But what seems most likely is that Old English became politically dominant, and was viewed by the Britons as being a prestige language, something they needed in order to be able to climb the social ladder of life and maintain their living standards. This is not dissimilar to my dad as a young man deciding to use General British over a less prestigious London accent such as Cockney in order to help him get a job in a bank. In fact, we still see people electing to speak English at the expense of other languages all over the world, for reasons which are not dissimilar.

Over time, the majority of the remaining Celtic Britons in England simply stopped using Celtic languages in favour of Old English, although pockets of Celtic remained in Cornwall and Wales. Many people living in Cornwall today are very proud of the Cornish language, and Welsh has become a revitalized language.

The linguistic legacy of the Vikings

The Vikings are probably the most glamorous and well known of invaders of Britain during the later Dark Ages, and places in Britain with any Viking heritage are usually all too happy to celebrate it. Replica Viking ships can be found in towns all over Britain, mainly on the coast or near waterways. For example, there is a replica ship called the 'Hugin' at Pegwell Bay in Kent, another at Unst in Shetland, one near Corrie on the Isle of Arran in the western Scottish islands, and sculptures in Largs on the Firth of Clyde in western Scotland and at Waltham Town lock near London. In Shetland, the annual 'Up Helly Aa' festival on the last Tuesday of January celebrates the end of the Yuletide period (modern Christmas), culminating spectacularly with a replica Viking long-boat set on fire, the gathered revellers singing the traditional song *The Norseman's Home* before heading off to party for the rest of the night. The best-known Viking-occupied town in England is York—Viking name, Jorvik, with the letter *j* pronounced like a *y*, as it is in Germanic and Scandinavian languages (and in phonetic script). There's a fascinating visitors' centre at York—the Jorvik Centre—which tells the tale of the Viking 'settlement'.

This celebration is all rather interesting, given many accounts portray the Vikings as generally intent on invasion of Britain on the bloodiest of terms. We used to use the phrase 'raping and pillaging' to describe the Viking war strategy; I don't know about you, but that does not seem like friendly behaviour! Even my mum was swept up in the romance of it all, saying how exciting it must have been during the Viking invasions, with all those big hunky guys 'raging and pillocking' all over the place, bless her. I have to admit, that might have been more fun. In recent history, we have been less keen to celebrate or embrace attempts at aggressive migration and annexation, wherever it occurs in the world.

The Vikings first invaded Britain in 793, getting to York in 866. They also invaded other areas of continental Europe and got as far as Iceland in the west, parts of Russia in the east, and Turkey in the south. We're interested here in what happened in Britain and how that influenced accents of English, but the Vikings who settled in northern France will come back into the picture in 1066. These are the Normans.

The Viking settlements in England were mainly in the east, encroaching on lands originally given to or taken by the Anglo-Saxons. This included regions now known as East Anglia, the East Midlands, Yorkshire, and Lancashire, but not Northumbria in the far Northeast. Anyone who has read Bernard Cornwell's *The Last Kingdom* series of novels, or followed the BBC drama based on it, will know Northumbria mainly stayed in the hands of the Anglo-Saxons. The extent of Viking settlement is known as the Danelaw, which divides the country with a line stretching from London to Liverpool. Figure 4 is a map showing this situation, somewhere between the ninth and tenth centuries AD.

The Danelaw corresponds closely with the modern A5 trunk road, originally a Roman road across Britain from London to Shrewsbury known as Watling Street. It also corresponds closely

Figure 4 Map of England showing the Anglo-Saxon Kingdoms and Danish Districts, produced *c.*1909

with some English accent features, the most notable being the pronunciation of /r/.

For example, up to the 1950s, most of the accents south and west of the Danelaw were rhotic. This means people with those accents pronounced an /r/ sound everywhere it is found in the spelling of words. There were a few pockets of this around Cumbria and Northumberland, which were not occupied by the Vikings (see Figure 4). Modern General British speakers only pronounce English /r/ before a vowel sound, not after it. In a word like *carrot*, we say the spelled *r* because there is a vowel sound after it, but in *car*, General British speakers don't. There are still speakers in the South—particularly the Southwest—and Northeast of England who pronounce the *r* in words like *car*, but this is dying out, and has more or less disappeared in most areas of England. In the 1950s, it was still common.

Figure 5 is another map, this time showing the production of /r/ in England in the 1950s, specifying where /r/ was produced everywhere it appears in the spelling. Pale areas are non-rhotic (/r/-less), and dark areas are rhotic (/r/-full). We're ignoring Scotland and Ireland in this image which is why they are white.

Just look at that pale, /r/-less area. It matches the Danelaw very closely indeed. That cannot be a coincidence!

The Vikings spoke a language known as Old Norse. According to Óskar Guðlaugsson's web page on the pronunciation of Standard Old Norse,[2] the language was non-rhotic. Old English, however, was rhotic. You can hear this in modern recordings of parts of the *Anglo-Saxon Chronicle* or the epic poem, *Beowulf*—which is actually a Norse story written in Old English. The YouTube video[3] accessed from the QR Code has pronunciations for the

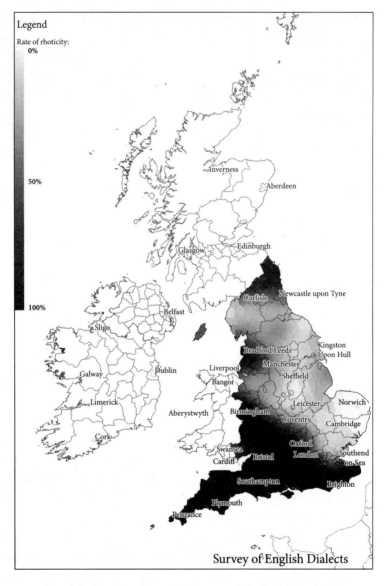

Figure 5 Rhotic and non-rhotic areas of England in the 1950s

names in *Beowulf*, and spelled 'r' is pronounced in names such as *Eofor* and *Unferð*:

Scan here or go to https://www.youtube.com/ watch?v=rbOSL0_Vs3c to hear pronunciation of names in *Beowulf*

If you listen closely to the /r/ sound in the recording of names in Beowulf, it doesn't sound much like modern English /r/. That's because the Anglo-Saxon /r/ was usually trilled. In Chapter 1, I mentioned the term 'rolling the "r"' to describe this, and it is a type of /r/ sound found in certain styles of singing, and if you're familiar with Spanish you'll have heard it there. The fact that we don't hear this type of /r/ in modern accents of English in England—let alone at the ends of words—is an example of sound change. We do, however, hear it in Scots.

The bottom line is that the British Isles' modern accent boundaries were mainly drawn by the Anglo-Saxons and the Vikings.

There are other things Old Norse brought the English language in terms of pronunciation. For example, etymologically, the words *skirt* and *shirt* refer to the same item of clothing. They come from the common root of both Old English and Old Norse, called Proto-Germanic. The word in Proto-Germanic was *skurtjon*, meaning 'a short garment'. The Old English word is written *scyrte*, the digraph (two-letter combination) *sc* being pronounced in a similar way to modern English *sh*. In Old Norse, it is *skyrta*. Eventually, the words came to mean different items of clothing, so we get double duty from this one word thanks to the Viking invasions. Similarly, the

47

name of the town *Skipton* in Yorkshire derives from *sheep* and *town* or *farm*, reflecting Viking-influenced pronunciation and the fact that Skipton had a strong association with sheep farming.

If you look at the first map (Figure 4), you can also see other boundaries, which are often natural features such as rivers and areas of high ground (if not exactly mountain ranges). These also correspond to some of the dialect boundaries you can see in Figure 5, many of which are still in place today. Again, this is probably because of restricted movement. Natural boundaries tended to confine people and make it difficult to move around and meet others.

It is estimated that the population of England and Wales was about 1,600,000 in 1000 AD (from around 100,000, including Scotland, in 750 BC), which is less than the modern population of the county of West Yorkshire. This means that England and Wales were still relatively sparsely populated at that time and people were still living in close-knit communities and didn't move around much. The fact that Figure 5 shows the situation in the 1950s is an indication that there was still a general lack of physical (and social) mobility up until that time. Improvements in fast transport links since the 1950s, like the building of motorways and proliferation of high-speed railway connections, have to a great extent brought the country together linguistically since that time. Where /r/ is concerned, for example, much less of England is now rhotic, and we could attribute that partially to the building of the M4 motorway, linking the Southwest of England with linguistically influential and non-rhotic London.

1066 and all that

In 1066, the Normans invaded England.

We think of the Normans as being French. They were, but they were French of Viking descent. The word *Norman* literally means 'north man', and Norman France was the area of France which had been settled by the Vikings (or Norsemen) around the same time as they were arriving in England and parts of Scotland. The area of France they settled in is known as Normandy. England's later Plantagenet kings, from Henry II (1154) to the end of the reign of Richard III (1485)—the king with scoliosis whose body was discovered buried under a car park in Leicester in 2012—were descendants of William the Conqueror and all spoke French, although the exclusive use of French among the ruling classes seems to have died out by 1300 when English was re-asserting itself. We call that variety of English 'Middle English'. When the nobility were using French and the working classes were using Old English, there was probably little mixing between the two languages. Once the ruling classes started to use English, many French words began to enter the English language—like *change*, mentioned earlier.

Norman French had an effect on how English was spoken, but it does not appear to have had much impact on regional accents. This may be because, unless you were from the ruling class and needed to go on progresses across the country to check your taxes were being collected efficiently, you were still highly unlikely to move away from your home town or village. Even if someone from the ruling classes did do a lot of travelling, the people they would most likely meet and interact with were not the *hoi polloi*. The mobility of the upper classes, however, eventually led to the formation of the accent known as Received Pronunciation (RP), which is a social rather than a regional accent and can be heard all over the British Isles.

Bringing it together

So, what have we learned? There are a number of themes coming through.

Firstly, English is not a pure language. The language we now think of as British English—the language of J. K. Rowling, Jane Austen, Shakespeare, Chaucer, and the Anglo-Saxon Chronicle—is a mode of communication which developed over hundreds of years and is the result of migration and invasion. People living in Britain now are all descendants of migrants from mixed origins... and the English language is a result of that.

Secondly, regional accent boundaries in Britain were put in place very early in the development of English, with the Anglo-Saxons and Vikings mainly to blame for a situation lasting up to the 1950s, and still in evidence today.

Finally, the seeds of the development of the upper-class accent, RP, were probably sown when England was ruled by a group of people who did not speak the local language as their first language, that is, the Normans. These people constituted the only group with the means and the need to travel widely in order to govern the country. While the descendants of William the Conqueror did eventually start using English along with French and Latin, the clear linguistic separation between the crown and its subjects is something which continued into modern society, albeit with the use of a different, non-regional accent rather than an entirely different language.

But to some, RP may as well be a different language.

Speech and tribes

Humans are tribal. We organize ourselves into distinct societies which follow a particular way of life, often for generations, and consider ourselves to be separate and distinct from other tribes, who are often seen as a threat, or as competition.

From an evolutionary point of view, the threat might well have been physical, with one tribe raiding another for possessions, produce, livestock, or even people in a show of superiority and strength, thus warding off the chance that they might be raided in return. We may believe that we are now living in a civilized society, with laws and penalties aiming to prevent such threats. However, humans still perceive tribal threats, whether or not the threat might be real, and continue to create competitive groups in an attempt to showcase strength.

Sport is a good example of this. Humans compete locally, nationally and internationally in sport, and competition between tribes can become quite heated.

Here's a fictionalized example of the impact of tribal competition in a setting you might not have expected. A man we'll call Frank Marshall had been a diehard fan of his local football club for as long as anyone could remember. When Frank died, he had left instructions in his will that it was his wish that people honour his lifelong attachment to the club by singing the song associated with it at his funeral service.

Despite their love and respect for the deceased, more than half the congregation refused to sing the song.

Frank's wife, already having difficulty holding it together, was distraught that family and people she had thought were friends of her husband would not carry out his dying wish. What harm would it do to celebrate the life of this person in the way he wished? Why wouldn't they sing the song?

I expect you can guess why. It was because they were supporters of another football club.

The dissenting members of the congregation refused to budge. They stood silently with their hands clenched in front of them and their eyes closed or raised to the ceiling of the chapel while the anthem was played. Some of them seemed affronted that Frank had expected them to sing it, as if it were some kind of final, distasteful practical joke by the deceased. Football meant more to them than family or friends.

That's a tribe.

People can of course belong to more than one tribe, particularly if those tribes are in different domains. For example, one might be a fan of a particular football club, and also a member of a dance society with other members who are fans of a rival football club. Discussion of football may never come up at the dance society, so you may never find out that someone you consider to be part of your tribe in one domain is a sworn enemy in another... until one day you bump into them wearing a different coloured football scarf at a match.

I experienced a similar feeling after the Brexit vote in 2016. People I count among my friends had voted differently from me. In the aftermath of the result itself, I went through something akin to the grieving process. When I discovered there were some people in my social networks who had voted differently from me, it was all I could do not to reject them.

Regional accents raise the same kinds of tribal feelings among speakers of a given language, and this is certainly the case in the UK. People who speak differently are 'not one of us', and this is a kind of threat which is probably a hangover from evolution and the need to protect your family and livelihood. Reactions can vary from the more or less imperceptible to the extreme, depending on the perceived level of threat the speaker poses. That threat can be a face threat—i.e., a threat to someone's self-image—as much as a physical one.

Here's a (slightly embellished) example from my student days, which I spent in York. One Guy Fawkes night (November 5th), I had some friends visiting from the South of England, and we decided to see if we could find a local bonfire and fireworks display. We read about one in the local paper and had to walk a good couple of miles outside of the city to find it.

It was brilliant. We paid a small entry fee on the gate, were given sparklers to hold, and stood around oohing and aahing at the fireworks with everybody else. There were hot drinks, and a jacket potato cooked in foil in the embers of the bonfire and served with baked beans or cheese and lots of butter. We felt very welcomed and included. Spirits were high. We were a temporary part of the tribe.

When the display finished, we thought we'd find a pub for a quick pint before heading back. There might even be an open fire to preserve the glow from the bonfire and warm us up again. Laughing and joking, we bustled into the nearest hostelry.

My experience of pubs in the city was nothing but positive, and it didn't occur to me a more rural pub might be different.

You know that scene in Western movies when the city boy arrives in a frontier town, pushes open the swing doors of the bar, and everyone stops talking and turns around and stares at him?

It was just like that. And the reaction of the people in the pub is a non-embellished part of this story.

Almost without exception, everyone in the pub turned towards the door and stared at us. The barman stopped halfway through pulling a pint. The person at the piano stopped playing. Even the pub dog stopped scratching himself to look at us. But we were cold, in need of a drink, in a good mood, and filled with youthful bravado, so we walked into the pub and up to the bar.

My friend Steve approached the bar and politely ordered three pints of local ale and a Coke. The barman stared back.

After what seemed like an age, the barman said, 'You don't sound like you're from around here.'

'No,' said Steve. 'I'm from London. Nice to meet you.' He smiled, winningly.

I was now expecting the barman to say something along the lines of 'We don't serve your type in here.' But he didn't. Barely losing eye contact with one or other of us, he served our drinks. Steve paid, and we went and sat quietly in a corner out of the way to drink them. Conversation in the pub, lively when we'd entered, remained muted.

We finished our drinks . . . and fled. I'll swear I heard the piano start up again the moment we left.

The situations I describe above with the actor, Alison Davies, my own situation growing up, and a group of southerners trespassing where they did not usually dare to tread, are not unusual.

In Alison's case, she changed her accent from something mildly regional to be closer to the standard. This was ridiculed by some. When she appeared to go back to something closer to her original regional accent, those people who had criticized her felt much more comfortable about this, but criticized her again for changing back.

Why should that be? Why does the way people speak matter so much?

We can look to tribal competition to answer this. One particular set of tribes in the UK concerns class. A person's accent is very much associated with their class background. Basically, the closer you are to RP, the more upper-class people believe you to be. If there is high-profile documented evidence—as there is with television personalities—that you have changed your accent, this is seen as an attempt to move from one class to another, usually by moving towards RP in order to sound 'better than you are'. This is perceived as a competitive move and, particularly among women, it seems, is not usually met with approval—even though women are usually at the forefront of linguistic innovation. It is important to know one's place in society, and to stay in that place if you are not going to be perceived as a threat.

But why should Alison be subject to more criticism for then changing back to something closer to that Liverpool accent?

The British love a failure, and love to laugh at a failure. We're clearly not the only nation to do so, as the Germans have a word for this: *Schadenfreude*, which means the enjoyment you get from seeing others fail. You thought you could climb the greasy pole of society, did you? How enjoyable it is to see you slide back down to the starting position, *where you belong*.

What a cruel lot we are.

Alison's example is to do with moving from a regional accent to a less regional one. Another kind of perceived tribal threat can be when someone moves from one region of the country to another. That's what happened to us in the Yorkshire pub; we southerners turned up en masse and it was not welcome. It may be more acute if there is a group of people, as it's seen as a kind of invasion.

This threat seems to be particularly problematic if the person involved is a teacher.

Teachers and accent prejudice

Teachers inhabit a potentially influential place in society. Indeed, the profession used to be very highly respected and relatively well paid; I'm sure there are teachers who would refute that now.

As the people who work to develop our intellectual, social, and practical abilities, teachers are often with us at key times in our development as people. I'm not the only one who has benefited from inspirational guidance from teachers in my life, and I don't know anyone who doesn't have a favourite teacher.

You might think that a teacher's accent was less important than their ability to convey complex ideas clearly and support the learning development of our young people. You'd be wrong.

Researcher Alexander Baratta[4] interviewed a number of teachers working in schools in Manchester about their accents. He found that teachers from the Midlands and the North of England felt under pressure from their teacher mentors to change their accents, essentially by making their accents sound less regional. In a related news story, a teacher from Cumbria in the North of England working in Reading in the South was told by the school to change her accent[5] following comments made by an Ofsted[6] examiner. This was actually set as a 'target' by the school to improve her performance. The implication in the article was that she might be out of a job if she didn't do something about her accent—that is, her Cumbrian accent made her unsuitable to teach in Reading.

As Baratta points out, there is nothing in the guidelines from the British government stating that teachers cannot have accents originating in different parts of the country from the region in which they are teaching. Teachers are required to promote 'the correct use of standard English' ... but it's possible to do that in a range of accents, not just in a prestige accent like RP. So why are teachers being urged to change their accents?

It's possible that there might be pressure from parents. This could be real pressure, or imagined. A school could perceive that parents are not happy that their children are being taught by someone with an accent different from the local one or different from one with higher prestige. As I've mentioned, accents are tribal, so if a teacher—particularly a favourite one—has an accent originating from elsewhere in the country, there could be the perception that the children would pick it up and this would distance them from their social group. There could also be a perception that a child's education is hampered if the child first has to work out what their teacher is saying. This could result in low satisfaction scores, or even in the child being moved to another school. This is not good for league tables...and, in Britain, the educational system is ruled by league tables imposed by the government which can have a bearing on how much funding a school receives. So, it's political.

It's also possible that negative comments made by parents about a teacher's accent could have an effect on the children's attitudes towards that teacher. In that case, a school or mentor recommending a teacher changes his or her accent could be doing this in what they feel is in the best interests of the teacher. If your dad or mum tells you a teacher sounds 'stupid'—because they sound different and that's threatening, or because their accent has negative stereotypes associated with it—then there's a good chance you will believe them. This will have a bearing on classroom engagement, how much the children respect the teacher, and could possibly affect learning outcomes—not because the teacher has a different regional accent but because negative attitudes cause people to behave differently towards others.

One teacher from Bristol in Baratta's study said he had changed his accent to avoid sounding like 'a village idiot'. That sounds more of a personal choice than one motivated by comments from a mentor or from parents, but it is still a judgement made because of our accent prejudices. Rural accents, including those coming from the West Country, tended in the past to be associated with farm labourers, and that stereotype still sticks. Speakers with those accents are judged to be uneducated, whether or not this is the case. Clearly, this is an issue for a teacher. If the teacher felt that the kids were unlikely to take him seriously because of his accent, this could lead to similar problems as we might see with parents telling their children a teacher sounds 'stupid', and might result in the teacher losing his job, let alone his self-respect and confidence in his ability to do that job.

But there is also another situation which arises: a teacher might sound too posh in a particular school. A primary school teacher friend of mine with a standard-sounding accent confided that she changes the way she speaks to be nearer to the speech of the children and less posh-sounding. She feels that speaking with her usual accent creates a sense of distance between herself and the kids. This is not what she wants as a primary school teacher. By adopting some of the accent features of the children she is teaching, she feels they perceive that she is more part of their speech community, which helps remove any barriers to communication that might impede learning.

Another friend of mine was telling me about a situation which is the flipside of this one. She's from the North of England, lives in the South of England, and has noticed that her son's accent is changing away from her northern one to be more like that of his teachers and classmates. Even the way he says his name has changed because of this. 'It's almost like he's not my boy any more,' she says.

How people are perceived through their accents

Let's revisit the comment from the teacher with a Bristol accent who said that he didn't want to sound like 'a village idiot'.

Some accents in the UK are perceived negatively, and some are perceived positively. That seems fairly straightforward, and you can probably name accents which you think sound 'better' than others, and those you think are 'ugly'. My father clearly thought

General British, or Southern British Standard, sounded better than Cockney, and that's why he adopted General British to get a better job, and insisted I used it for the same reasons.

But it's not quite as straightforward as that. People who speak General British (or RP) may sound more educated, but do they sound as friendly as someone from Bristol, for example?

In the 1970s, some ground-breaking research by sociolinguist Howard Giles[7] set out to test this. He had noticed people from around the country were judged differently based on their accents. The method he adopted is known as the 'matched guise' technique, originally developed in Canada in the 1960s by researcher Wallace Lambert and colleagues.

In the matched guise test, listeners hear a passage spoken in a number of accents and rate the speaker on things like intelligence, leadership, physical attractiveness, friendliness, trustworthiness, social status, and so on. They are not told where the accents are from or anything about the speaker, and not shown any pictures of the speaker. Each listener hears the accents in a different order so there is no regular effect of one accent on the next, and speaking rate in the recordings is kept constant, along with other things like volume and voice timbre.

Here's the clever bit. In order to make sure it is the accent and not other factors which are affecting listeners' ratings, the speaker they hear is actually the same person performing all the accents. Listeners are not told this.

Giles tested a number of accents this way. His main findings were that RP always came out top in terms of prestige ratings such as intelligence, authoritativeness, physical attractiveness, and social status, but did not do so well on friendliness, trustworthiness, or having a sense of humour. The Yorkshire accent and rural accents, such as those from the West Country and

Wales, were thought of as friendly and trustworthy but not educated or authoritative, whereas urban accents from Liverpool, Birmingham, and the Cockney accent were viewed unfavourably in terms of both aesthetic content and perceived status. The West Country accent did OK in terms of aestheticism, but poorly where status was concerned. You can see why the teacher from Bristol might want to change his accent if he was aware the Bristol accent is not perceived as sounding intelligent or authoritative.

But the issue here is that it is about the accent, not the person. In each case, the person speaking was one and the same. What the listeners were evaluating was not the person but the accent. It made no sense from a personality point of view that the speaker should be judged differently simply on the basis of his accent. And yet, that is exactly what happened.

Giles's work was carried out in the 1970s. It might be assumed that our opinions have changed since then, as we are much more likely to hear regional accents on the television now than we were in the 1970s—with the exception of the urban Lancashire accent, which has been on our televisions since the 1960s through the long-running soap opera *Coronation Street*. This, however, was originally a tale of working-class people, and the managers of the factory in *Coronation Street* did not have strong urban Lancashire accents.

Sadly, accent prejudice is still very much with us. I was asked to comment on a survey by a dating agency which had found that RP and the Edinburgh accent were the ones most preferred by those seeking a partner online. This is presumably because RP and Edinburgh accents are both high-status accents, implying a speaker is educated, and therefore has a good job. The fact that RP speakers are not viewed as friendly or having a sense of humour does not seem to be an issue for online daters.

Speaking of dating, researcher Gerry Howley recently wrote an article which appeared in the *Independent* on linguicism in Twitter posts.[8] She was commenting on the 2018 season of reality television show *Love Island*.

Howley starts by saying it was entirely predictable which of the contestants on the show would receive criticism about their use of English—and indeed it was. The person who got the highest number of negative comments had two things against them: 1) they were from Liverpool, which has an accent often criticized for sounding ugly; and 2) 'they' were a 'she'—and, for some reason, if you are a man with an urban regional accent, it is much less of a problem than if you are a woman.

Howley tells us that contestant Hayley's voice was described as 'annoying', 'cringeworthy', and that it made viewers' 'skin crawl'. One Twitter user then went on to question Hayley's level of education based on her accent. How fortunate for those annoyed, cringing, and shuddering viewers that Hayley was the first to leave the show.

The other contestant whose voice received criticism for being 'annoying' was Niall from … where do you think?

… the West Midlands, which is the region of England where Birmingham is located.

Another scandal to hit the news was about the pay differences of men and women at the BBC. Some women journalists have stepped down from roles comparable to those held by male colleagues because the women are not getting equal pay. Bringing an accent angle to this, BBC business news presenter Steph McGovern has claimed that she would be paid more if she had a 'posher' accent. As mentioned before in this book, Steph has a Middlesbrough accent, Middlesbrough being a city in between Newcastle upon Tyne and the North Yorkshire Moors in the

Northeast of England. Her stance is that the BBC is not doing enough to recruit people from different class backgrounds. She said that the management of the BBC is largely representative of the middle and upper classes and does not, therefore, know how to attract people from the working classes, who will more likely have regional accents. In support of Steph's point, some research by one of my undergraduate students revealed that secondary school students and teachers believe people with accents closer to RP are more likely to be hired after attending a job interview than those with regional accents, even when the regional accents are local to the company. My father had spotted that as a child in the 1920s.

I've noticed that the BBC seems to have more people with regional accents on the less formal news programmes, such as BBC Breakfast, since the pay/accents furore. This could be because the BBC moved their Breakfast programme from London to Salford near Manchester in 2012, but it seems only to have been relatively recently that we are hearing a greater variety of accents from the 'anchor' presenters on that show. I wonder if I'm imagining it.

In my case, the accent my parents wanted me to have set me apart from the other local children, and being 'posh' was a disadvantage at primary school. When we moved away from the terraced house and into a new semi-detached one in an area where there were more people with accents nearer to General British, I didn't stand out so much—at least not from the way I spoke.

Suddenly, I was one of the tribe.

CHAPTER 3

Men can't make their voices sound sexy, and other gems

L ois was really excited. She'd been on a number of dating websites for almost two years with no prospect of it going anywhere at all, and finally a match had come up on one of them which looked like it might have promise. She'd had a bit of gently flirting text banter with him and was beginning to think the two of them might be a good match.

They were trying to sort out a time and place to meet in real life (IRL).

In the meantime, they'd agreed to Skype on Thursday evening. This was a matter for great preparation for Lois, involving a lot of discussion on messaging apps with her friends about things like what to wear ('What would you normally wear on a first date, Lo?' 'It's been so long, I can't remember ...!' 'Avoid leopard print if you don't want to look predatory!'), whether to have her hair done ('Seriously, don't spend too much just yet.' 'Go for it! If you look your best you'll feel your best!'), and how much was too much make-up ('Ha ha, the trowelled-on look might scare him off!' 'Yeah, makes you look older anyway. Less is more').

She spent the week practising her opening gambit, working out the right head-and-shoulders position to adopt in front of the camera to show herself to best advantage, and trying out a new USB microphone. Clothes were strewn across the spare bed. She eventually decided she needed a trip to the local mall for a makeover, with her best friend Sally in tow—IRL, this time—for additional advice.

Finally, the time came. Lois sat down at the computer, taking care the camera and lighting wasn't giving her a double chin or that he could see up her nose. The makeover had used colours she wasn't used to, but Sally had assured her they took years off her and made her look slimmer ('Skype is ageing and fattening, you know—just like television.' 'What do you know about being on telly?!'), and Lois liked the overall look. She checked the settings several times to make sure all was well, and messaged him to let him know she was ready.

His image came up on the screen. Oh yes, he'd do very nicely! Very much her type from the way he looked. She could see him mouthing words, but there was no sound. He smiled and gestured apologetically—he could hear her all right! But he'd forgotten to switch on his microphone. And then the sound suddenly kicked in and they were chatting.

She realized something felt a bit wrong, but couldn't put her finger on it to start with.

Then she realized: it was his voice.

He didn't sound at all how she'd thought he would.

He had looked very self-assured in his pictures, and in his profile he came over as confident and intelligent. The way he spoke was really letting him down. His pitch was higher than she had expected for one thing, and he sounded oddly out of breath. It wasn't his accent.

Lois hadn't realized how important someone's voice was until this moment. Usually, when she met someone in person, she got the whole package at once. This technical glitch had made her realize that, if someone's voice wasn't right, it really put her off. He'd looked lovely for those first few moments of incorrect-Skype-settings-induced silence. Now she had considerable doubts whether she could take him seriously as a prospective partner—and that was all down to his voice. His voice had caused her to re-evaluate how attractive she found him.

She began to wonder how she must sound to him. She'd never really thought about that before. Was she coming over as too assertive? Did she sound just the right amount of sexy but still in control? How could she make her voice indicate that? And was that what he wanted?

Was her voice making him reassess her suitability for him?

Did it actually matter to him HOW she sounded??

The call finished, with a tentative agreement to meet up which was much less firm than Lois had originally planned—and the misgivings seemingly all on her side. She realized she felt a bit deflated. I'll stick to clean language here...

'Blast!' she thought.

Ronald (Ronnie) Kray and his brother Reginald (Reggie)—the Kray Twins—were identical twin brothers who terrorized the East End of London in the 1950s and 1960s through their organized crime activities. They were extremely well known to the British public for their gangland violence, and held celebrity status, partly because of their association with actors and artistes such as Barbara Windsor, Frank Sinatra, and Judy Garland.

On the BBC television programme *Saturday Kitchen* in June 2018, actor and musician Martin Kemp recounted how he met the notorious British gangster Ronnie Kray in prison before playing his brother, Reggie, in the 1990 film *The Krays*.

What was the thing that left most of an impression on Kemp after the meeting?

'It was the biggest shock of my life,' said Kemp, 'but Ronnie...'—he paused here for effect—'...had a really high-pitched voice!'

'You would expect him to have that voice like Danny Dyer in [British soap opera] *Eastenders*,' he went on to say in a gravelly, low-pitched voice. 'But he didn't! It was really up here!' mimicking Ronnie Kray's surprisingly high pitch.

This was clearly a surprise for Kemp. And I expect it would be a surprise to anyone who had met Ronnie Kray having previously only seen pictures of him or known about his reputation as a gangster. Just like Lois in the example above, we all have expectations about the way people will sound based on how they look and what else we know about them.

Physical size is often a predictor of how someone will sound.

But we also have expectations about how people will look based on how they sound. And this calls to mind an experience I had when I was a student.

As usual, names are changed to protect the innocent.

Back in the 1980s, I used to have a boyfriend who had—as far as I was concerned—the most wonderful voice. Just listening to him on the phone made me feel like everything was going to be all right. His voice was relatively low in pitch in comparison with other men and he sounded calm and confident. He sounded a bit like Daniel Craig in the Bond movies (this was looooong before Daniel Craig was famous). He was quite a nerdy guy, which I've also always liked—super-intelligent and fond of fantasy role-playing board games like *Dungeons and Dragons*. He had a ZX Spectrum computer when they first came out and we had hours of fun playing games on it, loading them from a cassette (many cups of tea were drunk while we waited). He was tall but relatively slightly built, glasses, no sense of fashion (sorry honey), and a haircut straight out of the 1970s (I may be exaggerating). We went to rock concerts together and watched science fiction movies.

I was talking on the payphone with him from my hall of residence once, and my friend Heather came round the corner. In the 1980s, I didn't have any choice if I wanted to make a call— a payphone it was. And payphones always seemed to be in the most exposed place possible in halls of residence. It was more or less impossible to have a private conversation, and soon my friend Heather was eavesdropping and hanging around making faces at me for being soppy.

'Heather says we're making her feel sick,' I told him, sticking my tongue out at her.

'Tell Heather I've got a bucket here if she needs it,' he said.

'He says he's got a bucket if you need it,' I repeated.

'Let him tell me that,' she said, grabbing the phone from me. Realization dawned on me that she was a bit drunk. It was 10 o'clock in the morning, so I suspected this was still drunk from last night rather than drunk in preparation for lectures.

They chatted for a bit before she handed the phone back to me and staggered down the hall to her room, but not before she'd given me a look indicating she was impressed with something about my boyfriend. I'll admit to being quite pleased about that.

'What was that look about?' I asked her in the canteen queue at dinner.

'Nice voice!' she said, piling roast potatoes on to her plate (I'll never know how she managed to be so skinny). 'Is he coming over so we can meet him??' She nudged me repeatedly with her elbow and raised her eyebrows at me.

'Unlikely,' I said. 'But here's a picture...'

I fished a photograph out of my bag where I'd had it in between the pages of my notebook and showed it to her. 'Isn't he lovely?'

Heather took the picture and grimaced at it. She held it at arms length to make sure she had focused on it right. She turned it this way and that. She even looked at the back.

It was clearly a bit of a shock.

'Is that him?' she said.

'Yeah.'

'Oh.' She looked disappointed. 'I was expecting someone more...hunky.'

'On what basis?' I exclaimed, and making a deliberate attempt to look affronted.

'I dunno. He just sounded...erm...' She waved her plate of food and cutlery round in her hands. 'He sounded...' She sighed, rolling her eyes, and gave up.

'Like he was built like a rugby player?' I supplied. 'You know that's not my type!'

'Yeah,' she said, deflated.

Oh, well. At least there wasn't much chance of her trying to nick him off me.

Men, women, and sexy voices

A study by Susan M. Hughes and colleagues in 2014 looked at whether men could deliberately make their voices sound sexy.[1] They hypothesized that this would be difficult for evolutionary reasons. But what are these evolutionary reasons? And were they right?

From an evolutionary point of view, successful male humans need to be visibly dominant, confident, and intelligent. This is mainly shown through physical parameters and prowess, such as strength and hunting ability, and being able to fight off competitors, whether this be through a meaningful glance, threatening stare, non-physical stand-off, or through coming to blows. Potential female mates are looking for someone who can father strong, healthy children, provide for the family, and protect the family against external threats. These could be threats from predators such as wild animals, but also from other tribes-people seeking advantage.

The voice is one indicator of how physically large and, therefore, potentially powerful a man is. Deep voices are created in physically large voice boxes, and it's often (but not always) the case that a large man has a large larynx. If you hear a deep voice but do not see the speaker, like my friend Heather, you make assumptions about what that person is going to look like in terms of size. The more physically powerful a man is, the more likely they are to be dominant and confident. This is what makes a man attractive as a potential mate, from an evolutionary point of view—and it will affect their voice.

Intelligence is not necessarily related to how deep the voice is. To be completely honest, I'm not entirely sure how this aspect works from a purely biological angle, so it could be more what you say than how you say it. In history, however, educated people have tended to come from wealthy backgrounds as, historically, those were the only people who could afford education, both from a financial and time point of view. As we've seen, certain accents are associated with wealth and education, whereas others are definitely not. While education is not necessarily a marker of intelligence, it is a societal marker. So, if you have a certain kind of accent which is considered to be prestige, or an accent close to it, people will assume you are educated and, therefore, intelligent.

Hughes and colleagues' study made recordings of twenty men and twenty women counting from one to ten. First, they were asked to count from one to ten in their normal voices. Then, they were asked to do it again four more times, each time intentionally changing their voices. They were asked to make their voices sound either more dominant, confident, intelligent, or attractive/sexy.

They were given some hints to help them achieve this. To sound dominant, they were asked to speak in a way that sounded assertive and authoritative. For confidence, they had to make listeners trust them and believe they were capable. In order to sound intelligent, speakers had to imagine they were delivering a presentation at an academic conference. And to sound attractive or sexy, they were asked to sound as if they were speaking to someone they were interested in starting a romantic relationship with.

The only thing they were allowed to say was to count from one to ten.

All of these changes to the way a person speaks will depend on a number of different parameters. Assertive and authoritative voices are likely to be relatively loud in comparison with sexy voices, for example. Changes in pitch pattern may also play a part, with wider pitch range at an academic conference, to indicate how interesting a subject area is and how much the listener should be engaging with it, and more narrow pitch range if someone is trying to sound confident and trustworthy, as this sounds less excited and more calm. Speed may also be a factor, with sexy voices tending to articulate words more slowly than assertive ones. And then there's voice quality. Those food adverts on television, featuring female voices almost dripping with the chocolate sauce you're seeing, are likely to be breathy in quality, as well being relatively low in the speaker's pitch range and slowly-spoken. This is basically using sex to sell the food.

But why get the speakers to count from one to ten?

The reason for picking something as mundane as this is to make sure the words used didn't have any intrinsic meaning which might affect listeners' judgements. If, for example, they had asked the speakers to describe something like a favourite childhood toy, different speakers could have used different language which could affect the outcomes. One might have said:

'I used to have a teddy bear.'

But another might have said:

'You know I had this gorgeous, plush teddy bear which I absolutely loved!'

The words somebody uses can say as much about their personality as their voice, so in research it is important to control for this by using something neutral, like counting from one to ten.

Once the voices had been recorded for Hughes's study, twenty male and twenty female listeners were asked to rate them on the four parameters (dominant, confident, intelligent, attractive/sexy). None of the listeners were exclusively homosexual, as the researchers felt this could have affected the ratings for attractiveness.

The results were fascinating.

For a start, the results from the listeners showed that all speakers were able to increase the impression of how dominant, confident, and intelligent they were by changing the way they spoke in comparison with their 'normal' voices.

However, only women were judged to have made their voices sound more attractive or sexy. Men's 'sexy' voices actually sounded less sexy than their 'normal' voices, according to the listeners.

This was true for listeners from heterosexual same- or opposite-sex backgrounds—that is, it didn't matter whether it was men listening to women, women listening to men, men listening to men or women listening to women...the results were more or less the same.

Does this mean it is true that men can't make their voices sound sexy?

Hughes and colleagues interpreted the results from an evolutionary perspective. I've mentioned how my friend Heather had dashed expectations about what my boyfriend would look like based on the sound of his voice. Hughes points out that there has been other research linking how attractive the voice is with face and body attractiveness. As men tend to be more concerned with physical attractiveness when looking for a mate, having a sexy voice can be a real bonus if you're a heterosexual woman. If your voice sounds sexy, listeners infer from this that you are going to be good-looking and (probably) physically healthy, therefore in a fit state to produce strong healthy offspring. From an evolutionary perspective, that is.

Women, on the other hand, are less interested in physical appearance (from an evolutionary perspective) and more interested in whether a man can 'provide' for her and their children. Hughes and colleagues linked this in particular to whether a man sounded confident. The women in the study rated men's 'confident' voices as sounding more confident than their 'normal' voices. Confidence is linked to a man's ability to earn money, to his social standing, and various other success indicators. This is more important to women than how good-looking a man is. Of course, if a bloke is gorgeous as well, that's certainly a benefit.

Let us re-examine what is meant by 'sexy'. For heterosexual men—and this is a huge generalization—it seems mainly to be down to how a woman looks. For heterosexual women—again generalizing—it is more to do with whether a prospective mate is 'successful'. In pre-monetary historical terms, this could mean fighting prowess as much as anything else, and so we're back to this notion of physical size...and physical size implies a lower average voice pitch. Heather's disappointment at my less-than-hunky (according to her) boyfriend, having heard only his voice, and Lo's puzzlement about her Skype date's voice having only seen him in pictures, are both linked to this. A man's voice can make him suitable as a mate, which can be sexy in itself, because they sound confident and successful...but men do not tend to make their voices sexy in the same way that women do.

There is another fascinating finding from Hughes and colleagues' study to do with confidence. While women rated men's 'confident' voices as sounding much more confident in comparison with their 'normal' voices, men did not rate each other's 'confident' voices as sounding that much more confident. The researchers suggest this is because men could be bio-programmed to deliberately downplay the confidence of competitors, observing that men tend to do each other down more than build each other up, a process they refer to as 'competitor derogation'. This competitor derogation is also more common than self-promoting behaviour. I wonder if this is because men perceive it is easier and more effective as a strategy to make competitors look bad than to make themselves look better. If you are able to speak in a confident voice that engenders trust, then presumably others are more likely to believe you if you put someone down by making derogatory remarks. We see this in politics all the time.

I mentioned earlier that women's voices in this study were perceived to make gains in dominance, confidence, and intelligence when they manipulated their voices from 'normal'. In particular, large gains were made where dominance is concerned;

women's 'normal' voices scored lowest overall on dominance, and both male and female listeners rated the 'dominant' version significantly higher. The score for 'intelligent' was also significantly higher. 'Confident' also scored more highly than 'normal' but—according to statistical measures applied in research studies—the difference was not considered significant.

Hughes and colleagues were surprised that women could manipulate their voices to be perceived as dominant in the same way as men. This is achieved mainly through lowered average pitch, making voices sound deeper.

So, what's going on here?

What could be going on is that, in recent times, women have moved into areas of leadership previously occupied by men, and have had to change a number of physical attributes to succeed in these domains (think shoulder pads in the 1980s). The researchers comment on the famous example of British Prime Minister Margaret Thatcher.

Anyone who has seen the film *The Iron Lady* will know that Mrs Thatcher has voice lessons in it. She's seen producing syllables on a slow, high to low pitch using a hand and arm movement, and being made aware of how authoritative her voice sounds when she calls her husband to account from across the other side of the room. The fact that she had voice lessons is a matter of record.

I've said that the average pitch for an adult male speaker is around the 100–150 Hz range, and for an adult woman it is in the 200–250 Hz range. There can of course be overlap in these ranges, and you get men with higher average pitch (like Ronnie Kray) and women with lower average pitch.

I've also mentioned that, when someone gets emotionally involved in something, their pitch range becomes wider. Often, wider is equivalent to higher average pitch.

Politicians and activists can be very passionate about things. One of the main reasons people go into politics is because they feel passionately about a particular cause and want to persuade others to see things the same way. How you say things can have a bearing on how persuasive you are. If you have a very wide pitch range, it can sound rather out of control and fanatical. In Mrs Thatcher's case, the combination of higher average pitch (being a woman) and increased pitch range (taking her into the higher reaches) meant that she was accused of sounding shrill, giving the impression that she was not in control. That's not what you want from a leader. I've demonstrated how uncomfortable that can be for listeners by giving one or two minutes of one of my lectures in a voice in my upper pitch ranges. Believe me, students have had enough of that very quickly! Female voices with lower average pitch are perceived as being confident, more trustworthy, and authoritative. I want to deliver my lecture in a way that students can listen to the message and be confident in it, and not give the impression that I am emotional (even though I might be), disorganized, and don't know what I'm talking about.

Mrs Thatcher had to change a number of things to be considered suitable for Conservative party leadership, and one of those things was her voice. Like the female speakers in Hughes and colleagues' study, she changed her voice to sound more dominant and confident. This involved lowering her average pitch and learning to keep her pitch range under control so that she, in turn, did not sound out of control. It also involved speaking more slowly. Unlike Hughes' speakers, she had to effect a permanent change, at least for her public voice.

But another interesting fact is that the sexy women's voices in Hughes and colleagues' study were also lower in average pitch than any of the other conditions. I'm wondering if there's a link here between the soothing, calming voices mothers use with children, which tend to be breathy and lower in pitch, the kind of voices men (and women) find attractive, and Mrs Thatcher's success in being elected as leader of the Conservative party and, subsequently, Prime Minister. Women's voices have to be authoritative and attractive in order to assume positions of power usually associated with men's roles. Men's simply have to sound authoritative.

Deborah Cameron draws similar conclusions in her March 2016 blog post 'The taming of the shrill',[2] although she points out that breathy voices—usually associated with women—also lack authority. The main thrust of the blog post (which is well worth a read) is that women's voices are criticized in a similar way to women's appearance, and that this is negative stereotyping. We saw that in the previous chapter, with Hayley from *Love Island* and Steph McGovern from the BBC.

Let's have a look at some of the other ways women's voices have been criticized, and myths surrounding them. We're moving now into the domain of vocal fry, or creaky voice, and 'uptalk'.

Women and speech

Young women are often held responsible by social commentators for introducing speech features older people find ugly or annoying. Women in general tend to be linguistic innovators, so it is not a surprise to see the blame laid at their door.

But is it fair to vilify only young women for using speech features such as uptalk or vocal fry? Are they the only people doing it? And what are these features, anyway?

Uptalk

Uptalk, sometimes referred to as 'high rising terminal', or HRT, is when the intonation of someone's speech goes up at the end of (mainly) statements instead of down.

Whether or not you've heard people's intonation going up at the end of statements, you may not have realized why it sounds different. Los Angeles-based media trainer Kim Dower described the impression uptalk can give as 'more like floating a question than stating a fact'.[3] English intonation uses differences in pitch direction to indicate whether a speaker is doing one of those things, among others. Here's a very short explanation of how this works so that you can see why uptalk has that effect.

Before I start describing intonation in English—which is one of my favourite things to talk about—I should just say that the description I give below is very, very basic. Intonation is quite a nebulous area, and I recommend further reading if you want to get into the nuances of it. I've produced some videos for my classes on intonation patterns in British English,[4] based on chapters in Peter Roach's very approachable book *English phonetics and phonology*[5]—you might find them interesting and informative. Alan Cruttenden's book *Intonation*[6] is probably the most comprehensive one out there on intonation in British English. There are links and references at the end of this book.

In British and American accents such as General British and General American, the intonation in statements is characterized by a falling pitch. This pattern indicates certainty, confidence, definiteness, and completion, among others.

Rising contours, where the pitch goes up at the end, are usually used to show one of three things: speakers have not finished; there is an element of questioning or request; or the speaker is inviting the listener to respond or participate—that is, there is openness in the conversation rather than closing it off with a falling intonation. Rising tunes are therefore associated with more speech to come, whether this is from the speaker or the listener. Where questioning is concerned, it could be a genuine question, such as 'Do you like popcorn?', or self-questioning to indicate uncertainty—for example, 'I like popcorn?' meaning I'm not sure whether I like popcorn or not.

Just to complicate matters, we can sometimes use a falling intonation on questions. The type of question most likely to have a falling intonation on it is known as a 'WH question', and starts with one of these words: *what, which, where, why, who,* and *how.* It is possible to have rising intonation on questions starting with one of these words, but that tends to be an echo question, that is, one which repeats the question again, often to check whether a listener has heard it right.

Here are some examples, with the direction of intonation indicated with an arrow.

Speaker 1 (genuine question): What time does the train come? ↘

Speaker 2 (checking what Speaker 1 said): What time does the train come? ↗ **(Statement):** Five o'clock. ↘

WH questions with rising intonation can also indicate disbelief or surprise:

Speaker 3 (statement): I put my car keys in the fridge last night. ↘
Speaker 4 (incredulous): Where did you put your car keys? ↗

Uptalk is where people use rising contours on sentences usually associated with falling ones, but there is no intended implication of not being finished or questioning. One suggestion is that speakers do it to include the listener and/or show social openness—that is, to establish communicative rapport. Whatever the reasons were for doing it in the first place, it has now become a common feature of many English speakers' speech. But people still associate it with younger women.

This phenomenon has been around for a while. There are references to it in novels such as John Updike's *Marry Me*, first published in 1976, and David Lodge's *Paradise News* from 1991. Both of these are set in the United States. People often think the British got it in the 1980s from Australian soap operas such as *Neighbours* and *Home and Away*, as it's certainly a feature of Australian English accents. We're exposed to so many different accents of English from all over the world these days that it's not really a surprise that features of the ones we're most familiar with rub off. Once people get used to a pattern of speech and start using it, others will adopt it too.

Many people are annoyed by uptalk, and make judgements of speakers who use it, just like they do with regional accents. It's even been suggested that it can have a negative effect on your job prospects. A survey of 700 UK company bosses published in 2014 found that they were prejudiced against uptalk in job interviews.[7] This is because, in the bosses' opinion, it makes the interviewee sound uncertain, insecure, and emotionally weak. The author of the report, which was funded by Pearson the publisher, concluded, 'If you know what you're talking about and want to be respected, then you need to sound like you know it.' To some people, uptalk does not sound like the speaker knows what they are talking about.

A report in *The Spectator* in the same year explained how students on a UK university Open Day for degrees in teacher training were warned not to use uptalk in their interviews.[8] If they did, they might not secure a place on the course. This could be interviewer prejudice, but it might also be because the interviewers feel teachers need to be in control of the class, and using uptalk may indicate weakness or uncertainty to the children. Intonation, just like accent, can potentially affect class control.

But is uptalk only the domain of younger women?

If John Updike had noticed it in the late 1970s, presumably these speakers are no longer 'young', and they may well still be using the pattern.

Paul Warren, Professor at the University of Wellington, New Zealand, has written an entire book on uptalk.[9] He notes that the earliest sightings of uptalk were in Australian English in the late 1950s, but that similar patterns have been observed in the English of New Zealand, Canada, the United States, the UK, Ireland, South Africa, and some other regions such as India and Hong Kong. Some research that I did on English in Hong Kong among speakers with a Cantonese language background also found uptalk, although not among many of them. Warren notes that uptalk in British English was recorded later than and, therefore, is more likely to have been influenced by Australian and American English. He also notes that there are some accents, like the West Midlands accent, which have a rising contour where General British would normally have a fall, but this is accent variation and not exactly the same phenomenon.

He also makes it clear that it is not something just observed among young women. While numerous studies have shown that women are more likely to do it, men do it, too—and increasingly so. As it is becoming more prevalent in society, and as women's position in society has changed since it was first reported, this may make it more acceptable for men to use it, particularly to show empathy with more senior female colleagues. Warren also notes how male-to-female transgender speakers use the stereotype that women use uptalk to 'pass' as female. There is more on transgender speech in Chapter 6.

Another matter discussed by Warren is whether only younger speakers use uptalk. Stephen Fry has reportedly associated it with 'the Sunny Delight generation', Sunny Delight being a fruit squash-type drink launched in the UK in 1998. As the pattern is normally associated with teenagers, if someone was a British teenager in 1998, at their youngest they will be thirty-three at the time of writing. There is evidence that older speakers use uptalk too, but most of it comes from Australia and the United States, where it has been a phenomenon for much longer. One American study showed that it was most used by middle-aged men, a group which definitely does not conform to the stereotype. If uptalk is a sign of being uncertain, it is possible to see how this might fit with the teenage years when personalities and social standing are being negotiated, but not with middle-aged men.

So, uptalk is more widespread than popular opinion would have us believe. And, what's more, the employers of tomorrow might well be using it, so may not even notice job applicants using it in interviews. But I expect by then there'll be some other speech phenomenon rubbing people up the wrong way.

When I did an online search for 'uptalk', other search items which were suggested included 'uptalk annoying' and 'how to stop uptalk'. I'm informed that British comedian Harry Hill has even written a song called 'I Wish My Brother-in-law's Voice Didn't Go Up at the End of Every Sentence'.

But another item also appears: vocal fry.

Vocal fry

If people dislike uptalk, they are really disparaging about vocal fry.

When I was little, I used to describe vocal fry—also known as creaky voice—as 'bobbly voice' (for example, 'Why has that man got such a bobbly voice, mummy?'). I'm a born phonetician, evidently.

One of my mother's responses would be that she expected 'that man' was tired.

From a physiological point of view, some people's voices naturally get creaky when they are tired. What happens is that the vocal folds vibrate so slowly that you can actually hear each vibration as a pulse of noise; it sounds bobbly (or at least, it did to me). I have said the typical frequency range for male speakers is 100–150 Hz—that is, the vocal folds vibrate 100–150 times per second. Creaky voice is more like 20–50 Hz. Ve-e-e-ry slo-o-o-ow.

The hatred for vocal fry on the Internet is quite startling. An article in *Time*, for example, describes it as 'droning' and 'world-weary'.[10] Another in the *Guardian* holds that it is the kind of voice quality a 'Valley Girl' might have after a night 'shouting herself hoarse at a rave', and claims some people think it makes women sound like ducks quacking.[11] Wikipedia describes it as a 'peer group affectation' among young women, and it is even suggested that women who use vocal fry are physically unattractive.

Do you notice—again—how a feature of the voice which is perceived as unattractive is associated with (young) women, making them, in turn, unattractive? Once again, women are criticized for a particular way of speaking. Once again, this is not really the full picture.

The recent research on creaky voice suggests that it seems to have begun as a phenomenon among young women in the United States, with reports of it starting to appear in the mid-2000s. But why are they doing it?

Researcher Ikuko Patricia Yuasa suggested in 2010 that younger women were seeking to give their voices greater gravitas by lowering their pitch considerably more towards the male register, the result being the adoption of vocal fry.[12] However, the attempt to sound more authoritative seems to have backfired, as vocal fry is listed as another of those features of speech which should be avoided in job interviews, as it is seen as annoying, and—like uptalk—gives the impression that the speaker is less competent and, therefore, less employable than someone who does not do it. (Women, you are damaging your career prospects by speaking this way! Etc. etc.)

This is probably not helped by the media personalities most associated with having vocal fry. Most often given as US examples are the Kardashians. In the UK, you hear it quite often on the television programme *Made In Chelsea*. One of my undergraduate students did her dissertation on creaky voice focusing on characters in *Made In Chelsea*, and found it was often used by speakers when they were trying to make themselves less threatening but also give advice, as in a love-triangle situation where a soon-to-be ex-girlfriend is giving advice to a soon-to-be new girlfriend. It was not just the women who used it, however; it was used by male characters too. Both the Kardashians and the cast of *Made In Chelsea* are glamorous, wealthy, and upwardly mobile (if not already upper class, in the case of *Made In Chelsea*), and this is attractive to younger people who, it is assumed, want to emulate them. The view of older generations can be quite the opposite, seeing these celebrities as time-wasting, self-absorbed, upper-class twits, and associating the voice quality with the personality.

In the UK, creaky voice is not a modern sociolinguistic phenomenon. It is also associated with old-fashioned RP, as spoken by upper-class adult males in the mid twentieth century. In the case of this group, it is considered to sound extremely authoritative and educated, fuelled by the associative stereotype that the upper classes usually had a public school education and went on to be involved in the running of the country. Modern speakers of this accent are few and far between, but British Conservative MP Jacob Rees-Mogg is an example. Whatever you may think of his politics, as a speaker he comes over as very confident, intelligent, and in control, and his vocal fry contributes to this impression. But there are still some who see him as a figure of ridicule, and his voice quality, if taken in modern terms, could have something to do with that.

In younger women, however, people have entirely the opposite impression if a speaker is using vocal fry. This seems to be a huge double standard. Is it because younger women are seen as affecting this voice quality in order to give themselves authority they (clearly) cannot have, being too young and, therefore, not experienced enough to have earned the right to sound 'world-weary'? And how exactly does it impact on how physically attractive they are?

Female commentators online, such as anti-sexual violence campaigner Marybeth Seitz-Brown, urge us to listen to the message rather than dismissing what women (in particular) have to say because of the way they say it.[13] Like Deborah Cameron, she points out that society regards female traits as shameful and something women need to apologize for, and the voice is included in that. Women are told to talk more like men (don't use uptalk; avoid vocal fry), but there is not a clear understanding among the general public of how such features of speech are used by a range of speakers. Stereotyping is rife, and voice prejudice is just as rife as accent prejudice. Vilifying women for the way they speak is a form of gender discrimination...and even of sexual violence.

The future of vocal fry and uptalk...?

The voice does matter, whether we like it or not. Expectations of how people should or will sound when they open their mouths to speak play a role in relationships, in our society, and in how well people get on in our society, whether there is any logic or fairness behind this or not.

I would like the message of this chapter to be that we should all be more tolerant of people's voice quality and pitch ranges. As a woman, I'd like to ask others who might judge female speakers—and it's often women judging women as much as men doing so—to realize this is a form of gender discrimination which contributes to other inequalities we see between men and women in society today. This is without bringing in transgender speakers...but there is more discussion of the transgender voice later in this book.

I'd also like to point out that the 'young' people using uptalk and vocal fry now are the older speakers of tomorrow, the speakers who will be in the positions of power in future—the bosses or university lecturers doing the interviewing; the newspaper pundits complaining about the awful way young people today speak. What will their voice prejudices be? Will they have moved away from uptalk and vocal fry, or will these features simply have become 'normal'? Will women have to continue to change their voices to be more like men if they want to assume positions of power and influence, or will there have been greater levelling between the voices of the genders? Language always changes... and differences in the way people speak will always lead to one group judging another, often not on favourable terms. I cannot see a time when there will no longer be innovation in the way people speak. And, as women are usually the leaders of this innovation, I cannot see a time when women will not be criticized for the way they speak, even if it is common knowledge that this eventually becomes the norm.

CHAPTER 4

'Gahaad save our Queen!' Professional and performance voices and accents

t's the British Grand Prix at Silverstone on 4 July 2015, and typical British summer weather (i.e. overcast). Dressed in white and with a marching band waiting patiently on the racetrack in the background, British R&B/garage singer and television personality Alesha Dixon stands on the tarmac, raises her microphone, takes a preparatory deep breath, and gives a heartfelt, earnest rendition of *God Save the Queen*.

 Scan here or go to https://www.youtube.com/watch?v=iGk2kkYpUVI to hear a sample of Alesha Dixon's rendition

The tabloid newspapers and social media explode with derision.

'"Gahaad save our Queen!"' shouts the *Daily Mail*. 'Alesha Dixon sets Twitter alight for singing national anthem at British Grand Prix with an American accent.'

'Alesha Dixon must be trying to make Independence Day a thing in Britain—that's the only reason we can think of for today's performance,' guffaws the *Daily Star*.

'Once you've heard "Gahahahahaaaahhhhhhhhd save the queen" there's no going back,' cries the *Daily Mirror*.

She has (apparently) murdered the national anthem.

As often happens on these occasions, phoneticians were asked to comment. I sat down with the recording and listened to the rendition. Had she really sung 'God Save the Queen' in an American accent? My colleagues and I were not so sure...

This chapter looks at a couple of groups of people whose presence is all about their voice—in this case, singers and radio presenters. It also looks in passing at differences between General British (GB) and the accent sometimes known as General American (GA). At the end, there's an interview with a voice coach, who supports performers' voice identities to help them represent characters (or themselves) accurately.

I'm going to start by looking at singers of (mainly) popular music, turning again to the thorny issue of accent. Yes, accent prejudice even creeps in here... and it's more to do with Brits trying to sound American.

British singers singing in an American accent

British and American English pronunciations have a number of differences. We basically have all the same consonants, but we use some of them slightly differently.

For example, a typical American English speaker will produce an /r/ wherever the letter *r* appears in the spelling. You may remember from Chapter 2 that accents that do this are called 'rhotic', and that most British accents historically had this feature; some still do. It is likely that the majority of modern American English speakers produce the /r/ because the variety of English spoken by the settlers who travelled there from the British Isles was mainly rhotic. While there has been a change away from rhoticity in much of England, the same change did not take place in America.

We also do rather different things with our /t/ sounds. At the start of words, they are similar. In the middles of words, however, they can sound quite different.

As mentioned in Chapter 1, many accents of British English use a glottal stop between vowels—the symbol for this is [ʔ]. In American English, the variant is not usually a glottal stop, but what's known as a flapped /t/, which has voicing (it's actually a tapped /t/, but that's splitting hairs). The phonetic symbol for that is [ɾ], but in the *Cambridge English Pronouncing Dictionary* we use the symbol [t] with a small [v] underneath it to show it is 'voiced'. You often see that convention in dictionaries. A flapped /t/ sounds a bit like a very quick /d/ sound, which is the voiced variant of /t/.

Let's use the name *Betty* as an example. Most British English speakers are likely to produce it as [beti], or [beʔi] for accents with a glottal stop between vowels. But if you listen to an American English speaker saying *Betty Grable* (the famous Hollywood movie star and forces' favourite from the 1930s and 1940s), or Barney Rubble from *The Flintstones* referring to his wife, *Betty Rubble*, they will likely pronounce *Betty* as [beɾi], with that very quick /d/ sound in between the vowels.

The symbol [ɾ] looks a bit like an 'r', doesn't it? In very posh and quite old-fashioned RP accents, some speakers used [ɾ] instead of /r/. If any reader remembers 1970s' British television sit-com *The Good Life*, posh character Margo Leadbetter would use it when saying her husband's name, which was 'Jerry'. She'd say [dʒeɾi], which sounds a bit like 'Jeddy', instead of /dʒeri/.

This is a very outdated-sounding pronunciation today in accents of England, but you'll hear [ɾ] for /r/ in varieties of English spoken in Scotland. The comedians Billy Connolly and Kevin Bridges, tennis player Andy Murray, former Manchester United manager Alex Ferguson,[1] and Mhairi Black MP have the sound before vowels, for example.

Some speakers of General British have what is known as a labiodental /r/, made with the bottom lip moving towards the upper teeth. The phonetic symbol for it is [ʋ]. Other labiodental sounds in English are /f/ and /v/ (see Chapter 1).

[ʋ] as a variant of /r/ was (and still is to some extent) thought of as a speech impediment, but actually it is quite common. Talk show host Jonathan Ross has [ʋ] for /r/, with very strong lip-rounding, and is known affectionately as *Wossy*. It's a feature of his speech which defines him and he seems quite proud of it. There's a clip of him pronouncing the name *Rachel Riley* on YouTube[2] and his /r/ sounds are very clearly [ʋ], even without the characteristic lip-rounding. Other famous speakers with this pronunciation feature include former Prime Minister Margaret Thatcher and comedian Paul Merton from BBC panel show *Have I Got News For You?* It does not seem to be as widespread in General American.

A last notable consonantal difference between General British and General American is how General American speakers pronounce the spelling *wh*. In General British, there is no difference in pronunciation between word pairs like *witch* and *which* or *wear* and *where*—but, again, we do find regional differences. In General American, however, the /w/ sound at the start of *which* is pronounced like you are whispering it, and so it is possible to tell words in pairs like *which* and *witch* apart out of context.

What about vowels?

While there are several vowel differences between General British and General American, the two I am going to focus on here are the vowels in LOT and BATH, using John Wells's standard lexical sets (see Chapter 1).

As with Northern British Standard accents—as opposed to Southern British Standard—the General American BATH vowel is the same as the one in TRAP. It sounds a little different as it tends to be quite long, and is often produced as a diphthong, especially before /n/. You may have noticed that the word *and* used as a filler when speakers are trying to think of the next thing to say can sound like *eeeaaand*, for example.

The tongue position for the LOT vowel in General American is similar to General British but, whereas LOT has rounded lips in General British, it has unrounded lips in General American. This makes General American LOT very similar to the Southern British Standard BATH vowel.

To summarize:

- General American LOT is like Southern British Standard BATH
- General American BATH is like Northern British Standard TRAP

I'm just going to pause here and draw your attention to the 'has unrounded lips' part. This will become important shortly when we consider Alesha Dixon's sung pronunciation of *God*—or 'Gahahahahaaaahhhhhhhhd', as the *Daily Mirror* would have it.

OK, so what was going on with Alesha Dixon's much-vilified rendition of the national anthem?

When I sat down to listen to it, the only thing which sounded particularly American was her production of *God*—as observed so keenly by the press. But—as my colleague Dr Erin Carrie from Manchester Metropolitan University pointed out in a BBC Berkshire interview—this might be more to do with the fact that Ms Dixon was singing the word rather than speaking it. And there are two reasons.

The first is that, when we sing a sustained vowel sound, it changes. In the case of *God*, sung powerfully at the start of the last line and over two notes as here, it is very likely that the singer will open his or her mouth wider, with the consequence that the lips become less rounded. Vowels with rounded lips are less loud than those with unrounded lips. If a singer is trying to get maximum volume into a word, as here, then unrounding the lips will help to do that. Do you recall I drew your attention to how the LOT and BATH vowels were very similar, but LOT has unrounded lips and BATH does not? And how the General American LOT vowel is similar to the General British one but has unrounded lips, so will sound like BATH? That's a possible answer for what is going on.

The second reason is that Ms Dixon is an R&B singer. R&B is an American musical style. I can't find any evidence that Ms Dixon was classically trained as a singer, so she sang the national anthem in the style she was most accustomed to: an

R&B style. If a singer sings a song in the style of R&B, it will sound American, whether or not the singer actually has many of the accent features associated with that style.

Listening to Ms Dixon's rendition of this song, she sounds very close to General British in every other respect. She even has the labiodental /r/, which is not common in American English. She does not sing with a rhotic accent—e.g., *her* in the line 'Send her victorious' does not end with an /r/ sound. In all respects other than the way she sings *God*, she does not have 'a dodgy American accent', which is something else the *Daily Mirror* said about her rendition.

In my opinion, the British press and social media were wrong to castigate her. And I wasn't the only phonetician to reach this conclusion.

Singers singing in other English accents: not just the Brits

This whole issue of Brits singing in an American accent has been around for A Very Long Time.

In popular music, the most often cited early gaffe from a British singer trying to sound American is when Cliff Richard sang 'Tell your mar, tell your par' (instead of 'Tell your ma, tell your pa') in his 1961 hit *A Girl Like You*. Cliff was styled as the British answer to Elvis in the late 1950s, and it was clearly important for him (and his agent) to adopt the stylistic and accent features of American popular music at the time to appeal to his fans. By singing *mar* instead of *ma*, he is doing something called overextension. Let me explain.

Most words ending with the vowel in *ma* and *pa* have an *r* in the spelling. Examples are *car*, *far*, *star*, and so on. Where there is an *r* in the spelling, this vowel is called the START vowel (see Chapter 1). In General British—being non-rhotic—we don't say the /r/ in START words, but Americans do. Overextension is when you add sounds to words, assuming they must be there when in fact they are not—that is, by analogy with other words having similar sounds. Hence, *mar* and *par*. It's that vowel, and it's an American accent, so it's got to have an /r/ at the end of it . . . right?

In this case: wrong.

We can see Eliza Doolittle doing overextension with /h/ in *My Fair Lady*. In the phrase 'In Hertford, Hereford, and Hampshire, hurricanes hardly ever happen', she drops the /h/ sounds at the start of *Hertford, Hereford, Hampshire, hurricanes, hardly*, and *happen*, which is usual in the Cockney accent, but she adds an /h/ to *ever*, which she produces as *hever* /hevə/.

But back to popular music.

A little later on in the 1960s, a rivalry emerged between The Beatles and The Rolling Stones. These two bands were at the forefront of what was known as the 'British Invasion' of the American pop scene in the 1960s. To succeed in America, they had to give the Americans (as well as the Brits) what they wanted.

The Stones were very much in the blues-rock tradition (still are), and tended to sound quite American. In fact, I thought they were American, until I was firmly put right by my secondary school music teacher in the late 1970s. The Beatles, on the other hand, were much less blues influenced, and more influenced by skiffle and beat music. Blues, skiffle, and beat are all American musical genre types. While both bands observed rock and roll influences, they sounded quite different.

They didn't sound different just because of their musical styles. Another reason they sounded different was because The Beatles sounded much more British when they sang. You could even hear the Liverpool accents on occasion. But they didn't start out like that. If you listen to *I Saw Her Standing There*, which is the first song on their debut album *Please Please Me* in 1963, you can clearly hear American English pronunciation features. By the time we get to 1965's *Taxman*, they're sounding less American— but still a bit—and 1967's *Strawberry Fields Forever* has very little in the way of American accent features. In *Strawberry Fields Forever*, you can clearly hear the /g/ at the end of *living* and *nothing*, which is a feature of the Liverpool accent, and no trace of an /r/ at the end of *forever*. That's not to say there were no American accent features in their songs at that time, but there were certainly fewer.

Neither The Beatles nor The Stones spoke in American accents. The Beatles had much broader Liverpudlian accents than the ones they sang in, and that sometimes puzzled the American media when they were interviewed. Mick Jagger's singing delivery was closer to GA, and he had more of a London-sounding accent.

This situation of singers singing in different accents from the ones they speak in is still going on, as we saw with Alesha Dixon. And it seems to be more down to musical style and genre than geographical origin. In a fascinating podcast, 'Faking the funk: singing in other accents',[3] American producer and reporter Nina Porzucki—who also thought The Rolling Stones were an American band—quizzes co-presenters Patrick (with a British accent) and Marco (with an American accent) on where various musical artists come from, based on the accent they are singing in. Las Vegas band The Killers are incorrectly identified as British (or maybe Irish), based on singer Brandon Flowers's vocal rendition, and Paolo Nutini—whom Patrick suggests is someone 'trying to sound American who is not American'—is judged to be either from Germany or South Africa, but turns out to have a very strong Scottish accent when he's speaking. But Patrick is right: Paolo Nutini is not American. These artists are from different musical styles, The Killers identified as 'indie', 'alternative', 'post-punk', or 'new wave', all of which have predominantly British origins. Paolo Nutini is more down the R&B end of the spectrum, and also has jazz influences—both of which are more stylistically American—with a bit of reggae thrown in (Jamaican). I'll leave you to listen to the podcast and see if you can spot the others.

Performing popular music is just like any kind of performance. In order to produce the songs effectively for the genre they were written in, a singer has to adopt a singing style which goes with that musical genre. If I were to sing the Country and Western song *Stand By Your Man* in a Southern British Standard accent (you can hear me doing this on the 'Faking the Funk' podcast), unless I were doing something very different with it musically, it would sound very strange. My father might disapprove if I was singing in an American accent—and oh boy did he disapprove— but it needs that accent for the genre. It's a bit like putting on a different hat for a different purpose; you could wear a straw sun hat to go horse riding, but it wouldn't give you much protection if you fell off.

What do singers say?

I'm fortunate to have one or two singers in my social circle. I asked a few of them about their singing voice versus their speaking voice, and what they do when they're singing in differ- ent genres. I'd like to thank them here for agreeing to be inter- viewed, and for the fascinating glimpse into their vocal lives.

Nicole Allan, from the band Stereo Snakes, is a singer-songwriter who also hosts various open mic nights in Reading and Basingstoke. Her genre? Country music.

'People are often quite surprised by my speaking voice if they've heard me sing,' she says. They expect her to be American and come from the Deep South because she sings Country. In fact, she was born and raised in Spain, speaks fluent Spanish—'with a local Malaga accent'—as well as very British-sounding English, and has parents from Scotland and Middlesbrough. When Nicole spent time performing in the United States, it was often a real shock for Americans to find out she was actually British. She's rather pleased about that, because she feels it means she's representing the genre well.

Nicole admits to being a bit of an accents chameleon, picking up the accent of the person she's talking to at the time. I explain that this is called accommodation. 'I go Scottish when I'm drunk!' she confides, with a giggle. That might be accent influence from her Scottish dad, I suggest. Nicole looks pensive while she considers that possibility.

Like my dad, Nicole's parents had rather firm views about the way she spoke. Her mum had moved from Middlesbrough to Kent before she met her dad, and has told Nicole that she had consciously changed the way she spoke to fit in. Nicole explained how her parents had influenced how she speaks. Her mum told her off for 'going American', and she has the impression her parents really didn't want her to sound like she came from the United States. When she speaks, she does not sound American.

Something I find interesting is that, while it can be a very strong indicator to many, Nicole believes accent is not a massive part of her spoken identity. This might be because she was not raised in the UK and so does not have the same kind of accent loyalties and prejudices, even though her parents have views on the matter. Her singing voice and accent are much more important to her, and it is essential for Nicole that she both sounds distinctive and fits the genre.

'I love it!' she says. 'I like that people know it's me the moment they hear my voice, even if they can't see me. I'd be offended if I was told to sing in a British accent. It's just not normal.'

This reinforces the notion that it is a style thing as much as an accent thing. Nadie Keating, singing coach and vocalist—and someone with an extremely impressive vocal range—seems to agree. 'Americanized singing has transformed how we use our vowels,' she claims. It's not that singers consciously pick a certain vowel; it's that that vowel will go with the style or genre a singer is singing in. A type of voice quality in singing popular music known as 'twang' is prevalent, and is typical of American genres such as Country, Blues, Soul, and Rock. A twangy British singing accent is going to sound quite American.

But you do also hear British accents coming through in some musical styles, often deliberately so. Nadie gives Cerys Matthews from Catatonia (Welsh) as an example, and I volunteer the Proclaimers (Scottish) and Damon Albarn from Blur (London), which was part of the 'Britpop' movement starting in the 1990s. Nadie points out that Albarn is actually quite posh and so it's more 'Mockney' than Cockney. But the accent he chooses to sing in is making a point about Britishness, and some of the themes in songs by Blur (for example, *Parklife* and *Country House*) had very British themes. This harks back to songs from the 1960s by The Kinks, who sang in a London accent about British themes, like scenes around London (*Waterloo Sunset*), 1960s nightlife (*Lola*), and the idle rich (*Sunny Afternoon*).

'Singers do what works for their larynx,' says Nadie. If you find your voice is more suited to a rock than a classical style, it will probably be inherently twangy.

One performer who feels very strongly about representing himself as English through his vocal delivery is progressive rock singer, guitarist, and producer, John Mitchell.

'Everything about me—my identity—it's very English. Singing in an accent that didn't reflect that would be a fallacy. Everything I love in terms of pop culture is English. With very few exceptions.'

John makes a conscious effort not to sound American when he's singing, as that simply wouldn't fit the progressive rock genre—and wouldn't represent him for who he is. For those readers who are not aware of progressive rock, we're talking about bands like Genesis, King Crimson, Marillion, and It Bites. John currently fronts It Bites, plays guitar in another progressive rock outfit called Arena, and is involved in several other projects, including his own Lonely Robot albums.

'OK,' he sighs, 'I'm going say it! And you can publish it in your book...I'm a bit of a snob about it. I don't think Americans should be allowed to make progressive rock albums.'

That's a very strong statement! I ask him why not.

'They miss all the important things about it. The irony. And the humour. The quaintness of it. Prog is a vision of an idyllic England that doesn't really exist. British people get that. Cucumber sandwiches. Garden parties.' I offer croquet on the lawn, Punch and Judy, and Knights of the Round Table.

So, prog should be sung in a British accent?

'Prog needs to NOT have an American accent,' he stresses.

John is another person who was made very aware of the way he spoke at an early age. His parents educated him at public (i.e. fee-paying) schools and sent him for elocution lessons. He has also had classical singing lessons. His mum was very keen that he should learn to speak properly. 'When I'm representing the family—representing mum—I'm very careful about the way I speak,' he tells me. When he does interviews for magazines, 'out comes "RP John".' He smiles, wryly. 'It's almost an act. I feel like I bellow a lot more!' And in the studio, when he's recording bands? 'Well, you accommodate, don't you? You want to blend in and sound a bit more rough and ready. Like the teacher friend you were telling me about' (see Chapter 2).

Something else John mentions is that for him to adopt another accent when he was singing would be a denial of his roots. I point out that, in a recent clip he posted on Facebook, he is heard singing with a rhotic /r/. 'Yeah, but I'm referencing the original,' he says. When he writes and performs his own material, it has to be sung in a British English accent. That's his identity. That matters.

I met another singer friend of mine, Andrea Ojano, when he was in a Bon Jovi tribute band. Now he's performing with a Foreigner/Journey tribute act. This is a very different situation from John's, as the 'voice' is never really going to be Andrea's own in this situation. We talk about the need to emulate different singers if you're going to produce a good tribute sound. It's very clearly about the whole physical presence for Andrea and not just the voice.

'It's not so much the accent. I try to replicate the emotions,' he explains. 'That really helps to get the voice. I look at the face and also how the singer moves.' Andrea talks about capturing the nuances of the voice of different singers, and how being able to listen analytically (he doesn't call it that but it's what he does) and reflect on his voice helps to hone his performance.

We also talk about his singing voice in comparison with his speaking voice. Andrea is Italian, from Sardinia. When he's speaking English, you can hear his Sardinian accent coming through. It's more straightforward to 'do' an accent with a song than when speaking.

This is probably because learning a song basically involves mimicry, or learning by rote. There is a lot of repetition in many songs, and this, along with rhythmic phrasing, helps the brain remember the lyrics. I was able to recite Dr Seuss's children's book *The Cat in the Hat Comes Back*, which is written in verse, from start to finish when I was little, before I could read, because I loved the story so much and my mother used to read it to me all the time. Multiplication tables are like this; while they don't rhyme, they have a definite rhythm to them and lots of repetition. One of my secondary school friends suggested learning German dative prepositions to a beat, and it really helped me remember them—'mit (rest), nach (rest), von, zu, aus (rest), bei (rest), zeit (rest), gegenüber, außer'.

If you learn a language event by rote like this, it releases your brain from some of the processing it needs to do and gives you more capacity for focusing on getting the sounds right. This is very different from speaking a language spontaneously in a communicative context, when a meaningful message has to be produced on the spot. As we saw in Chapter 1 with the speech chain diagram (Figure 1), there are a lot of processes that have to take place to produce spontaneous, communicative speech, and the brain is involved in coordinating all of those. If you are repeating something you've learned by rote—or singing a song you know well—rather than attempting to communicate something novel, you're using your brain differently, with less emphasis on the more 'linguistic' elements. The processing power you would normally use to formulate a new message in spontaneous speech can be directed to other aspects, such as pronunciation.

What this sometimes means is that speakers of English as a second or foreign language—like Andrea—get to the point where their English is well enough understood and then their spoken language pronunciation doesn't change much after that point; they keep their foreign accent. This is called 'fossilization', and could be because they like having some of their first language identity shining through, but that's not always it. As far as sing-ing goes, however, that's not good enough for Andrea—and not needing to direct brain power to the message allows him to focus on the pronunciation, helping him sound more like a native speaker of English when he is singing.

'It's more important to put an effort into pronouncing words correctly—not just replicating sound,' he says of singing in trib-ute bands.

But this has had an interesting knock-on effect for when he sings originals. He wants to sound like himself with some of his Sardinian accent coming through; to express his identity and background, like John Mitchell does. But he says he finds it hard to step away from sounding like Jon Bon Jovi! If you learn from the master . . .

'My voice is everything': radio presenters

So far in this chapter, we've looked at singers, and how they modify their accents to sing in different musical styles. But there is one group of people in particular who are more often heard and not seen: radio presenters.

Of course, with the Internet and social media sites, it's much easier now to see what radio presenters look like than it was in, say, the mid twentieth century. Some radio stations have webcams so you can even watch as you listen. Many radio DJs appear as presenters at live events, and some often have a television presence too. But the voice remains a very important element of a radio presenter's personality and identity.

Darren Redick is a DJ on Planet Rock Radio. He is from the United States, and talked with me about being an American in the UK and the choices he has made about his voice. He arrived from the States in 1991 with his British wife, and muses on a decision he made early on about whether he should try to sound more British.

'I was having an internal conversation with myself about whether to sound more British. There was an American guy at the supermarket checkout in front of me just when I was thinking about this, and I heard him say the very British phrase "Cheers, mate!" There was something not right about that. I know who I am, so I made the decision not to change the way I spoke.'

'My voice is everything,' he goes on to say. But that doesn't mean he necessarily has a very positive view of his own voice. He describes it as sounding like a cross between Woody Allen and Bobcat Goldthwait (from the *Police Academy* movies). I had to look up Bobcat Goldthwait. Darren does not sound like either of them. So, what does he think he should sound like?

'What you want to hear when you put those headphones on is, hey, this really sweet guy with a little bit of gravel in the voice. Like I've had too many beers and drank a pint of sand as well.' I remember listening to an advert for a Planet Rock-sponsored event which I was sure must be Darren's voiceover from the accent features, but had a lower average pitch. He confesses he recorded that ad when he had a particularly bad bout of laryngitis, but he was quite pleased with the result—presumably because it sounded like he'd had too many beers and had drunk a pint of sand!

Darren's been in this business for over twenty-two years as I write, but still doesn't sound the way he'd like to sound.

'When you're talking live on air, your microphone is going through a processor which is feeding back into your headphones and so you do get this full voice. But when you go back and listen to your playback, you just sound like you... and you sound like you do on your answering machine. You know, where you're hoping you're going [puts on low, slow breathy voice] "hey yeah this is Darren Redick", you're actually going [puts on higher-pitched, fast modal voice] "hi, this is Darren Redick!"'

We discuss what he calls 'craft'. He says how he talks is a slight caricature of how he sounds normally; he modulates his voice to be entertaining and engaging. This is second nature, he says, but he's very aware that he does it. He has what he calls a three-stage approach to chat between songs:

1. Come off the back of a track in semi-big radio presentation style.
2. His voice then drops down in terms of pitch range and average overall pitch to a more conversational tone for a story or comment.
3. Finally, he gets into the next thing (a song, adverts, or traffic/weather) by going back into radio presentation style.

I'm just listening to his show as I write this and he has actually done just that. He comes off a Guns N' Roses number by reminding the listener who they've just heard, into a bit of 'between you and me' chat about a time he saw the band and their hotly anticipated appearance at the Download festival (in 2018), and then his pitch jumps and the tempo increases to indicate we're moving on to the next thing after the advert break—in this case, traffic and travel.

Darren's wife is present when I'm interviewing him and she makes a rather interesting comment. Apparently, his daughter has said that his voice is very calming, and she likes to talk to him if she needs to calm down. 'She never said that to me!' he exclaims—and then admits that's a real compliment about his voice. I hope it will make him like it more.

Another Planet Rock DJ, whose main job is with talkSPORT Radio, is Ian Danter. Dants, as he is known, has an interesting story about how he got into radio in the first place—and it's all about his voice.

'I got into it by accident, really,' he says. Interested in radio since he was at school, Dants had been on a sixth form visit to the BBC when they told him he'd need a degree to get into broadcasting. But in 1997—and no degree in hand—an opportunity presented itself.

'I used to mimic football managers down the pub to amuse my mates,' he explains. One of those mates wrote a letter about his vocal impressions to the sports desk at BRMB, which is now Free Radio Birmingham, and suggested they have him on to do a spot. It must have been a good letter. On spec, they invited him in. He recorded a sketch in early 1997, and got asked in to record more. They then started paying him for the sketches, and eventually offered him a job as the Flying Eye, doing live traffic updates from a helicopter.

So much for needing a degree.

I'm always envious of people who can do impressions. I'm rubbish at accents too.

'Impressions take a while to mature,' he tells me. 'One word can unlock someone's voice.' He gives the example of famous British footballer Trevor Francis, who he describes as having a 'Plymouth burr'. Which word unlocked Trevor Francis's voice? 'It was *crossbar*. Once I'd got that, it unlocked the whole accent. With David O'Leary's southern Irish accent, it was *toast*.' He rolls the word around on his tongue.

Dants describes his own voice as having a Midlands 'tinge'. He feels very strongly that he doesn't want to sound very different on the radio from how he does off it, and that, while he doesn't want to sound too broad, he's been careful to keep some Midlands elements in his speech. He's thought very hard about how his voice represents him and doesn't want to sound too dour, which is how he thinks some West Midlands accents can come over. His voice is not typical of a Midlands voice, though. I ask if his accent has ever been a problem in his job—whether he's been subjected to accent prejudice. 'Well, they keep giving me work!' he replies, with characteristic upbeat cheerfulness.

We talk a bit about stereotypical British DJ speech, as mimicked by comedians Harry Enfield and Paul Whitehouse when they created Mike Smash and Dave Nice—aka Smashie and Nicey—in the early 1990s. These characters were based on BBC Radio 1 DJs of the 1960s and 1970s, such as Tony Blackburn and Alan 'Fluff' Freeman. Dants says he would rather be accepted with his current voice and accent than alter it to please someone or fit in with a stereotype of what a DJ should sound like. He calls this kind of accent 'mid-Atlantic' and says he is conscious to avoid it. He doesn't want to be a caricature.

One of the features of the speech parodied by Smashie and Nicey is something called denasalization, which is when nasal consonants /m/, /n/, and /ŋ/ are produced to sound like their plosive equivalents, /b/, /d/, and /g/. It can sound a bit like you've got a cold. I'm reminded of a Twitter exchange I had with Dants on the subject of stereotypical DJ voices, reproduced in Figure 6.

Like Darren Redick, Dants is aware of changing the way he uses his voice while he is on air, and he likens it to painting a picture. He definitely agrees that his broadcast voice is more animated than his non-broadcast voice. Commentating on cricket is very different from commentating on football, for example, and within any single commentating event there will be changes in tempo, volume, average pitch, pitch range, and voice quality. These have got to match the speed and excitement of what you are seeing to give the listener an audio picture of the event so they can visualize it in their mind's eye. One of my undergraduate students did a comparison of tempo, volume,

Figure 6 Twitter exchange showing stereotypical denasalization among DJs

average pitch, and pitch range in sports commentaries for tennis, golf, and football, and found football commentary to involve the most extreme changes. Dants agrees with that.

On Planet Rock, Darren Redick and Ian Danter spend most of their time doing links and fills between playing records. Dants's work on talkSPORT is pretty much non-stop commentary with a bit of banter with co-hosts. Neither of them reads the news.

So, what about a radio newsreader?

In 1943, in an interview with BBC Presentation Director John Snagge, he was asked why BBC radio didn't have women reading the news. Snagge explains that he did have Elizabeth Cowell—the first female television presenter and continuity announcer—read the news on one occasion. But, while 'a great many people would like [to have a woman reading the news], a great many would not'. He concluded that, in 1943, it was not time to reopen the controversy. It was not the time to 'put women on to this work'.

We are no longer in that position, but it has not been an easy road for female newsreaders. Nan Winton, the first female BBC television newsreader, read the Sunday evening bulletin from 1960 until 1961, when she was removed following negative viewer feedback on the acceptability of a woman reading the news. This was despite the commercial television news, ITN, having a woman—Barbara Mandell—from 1955. It wasn't until 1975 that Angela Rippon started a much longer spell as a newsreader on BBC television but, even then, the public seemed much more interested in her legs—hidden behind the news desk—than how well she read the news. This culminated in a comedy sketch featuring Rippon dancing on the *Morecambe and Wise Show*.

But back to radio presenters.

In May 2018, I was fortunate enough to act as guest editor on the Andrew Peach breakfast show on BBC Radio Berkshire.

Andrew's show was running a week of female guest editors in celebration of International Women's Day. They asked me what I wanted to talk about. My focus—predictably—was on different aspects of how people speak, including accent prejudice, and the experience of transgender people (more on this in Chapter 6). We also talked about whether English would continue to be used in Europe after Brexit...but that's a topic for another book.

We interviewed television and radio personality Adrian Chiles, who has a Birmingham accent and said he thought it was highly unlikely he'd ever be reading the news on the BBC. We discussed BBC television presenter Steph McGovern's comments about being female and having an identifiable regional accent, and how she felt both of these aspects played a role in the kinds of jobs she was given.

The newsreader on the Andrew Peach show was daytime programme presenter, Sarah Walker.

To start with, Sarah came in just before news bulletin time, sat down next to me, and then read the news. She did this in a fairly General British-sounding accent. The first time she did it, she simply left the studio immediately afterwards, reappearing for the next bulletin. But, after a while, she got drawn into the conversation—probably because I described her voice as 'smooth and chocolaty'. I thought it was exactly the sort of voice you'd expect to hear reading the news: authoritative and calming. Like it was saying: 'This is what's going on. It may be worrying...but it's me telling you, I'm explaining it to you clearly, and everything's going to be all right. No need to be alarmed.'

In conversation, her voice was a little different. For one thing, instead of having a BATH vowel in *last*—as she did when she mentions Reading's Bath Road in the news bulletin, for example—she produced the word with a TRAP vowel. I wondered whether this is evidence of the slow march south of the TRAP vowel in BATH words, as shown in the wonderful accent and dialect maps from the University of Cambridge.[4] I buttonholed Sarah for an interview.

'I'd describe my voice as fairly middle-English with a slight East Midlands twang,' she says. She hails from Leicester in the East Midlands, but feels her regional accent has almost gone after nearly twenty years living in the South of England.

'I've thought a lot about my accent, and I'm very mindful of how I speak, particularly when I read the news. I want the facts to speak for themselves, so I tone down my accent.' She does not want any of her regional speech features to distract the listeners so, even though she says she has not been told to do this, she makes an effort for her East Midlands accent features not to come through. 'A news setting is not about the person reading the news,' she tells me. 'It's about the news itself. I don't want someone to be thinking: "That's a funny accent" or "That's not an accent from around here". It would distract from the message.'

We talk about her BATH vowel—specifically from a news-reading point of view.

'I think I probably would say /bɑːθ/ (bath), or /grɑːs/ (grass)—but I might say /ˈtrænspɔːt/ (transport)' (with the TRAP vowel in the first syllable). I confess that I also have that pronunciation of transport—and I'm from Kent.

There are some words in particular that Sarah feels have got to have a southern-type BATH vowel. 'I always say /ˈkɑːsl̩/ (castle) rather than /ˈkæsl̩/,' she tells me. 'Windsor /ˈkæsl̩/ seems to grate quite a lot! So it's funny—there will be certain words that really stick out.'

How does this compare with the way she speaks in different radio settings? Sarah thinks there are three main modes for her voice on the radio: reading the news, presenting her own programme, and reacting to Andrew Peach when she gets drawn into the chat after her news bulletins.

'As a presenter, if I were to obsess over my accent, it would stop me from being the real me—and being relaxed enough to be the real me—and so that would have detrimental effects on who I am as a presenter.' When she's reacting to Andrew, though, she feels her voice is the most natural. I expect this is probably because she is more like a guest, not at that point responsible for any of the content but doing what anyone does in a conversation, along with all the additional processing the brain has to do when producing spontaneous speech. With news reading, the script is already prepared, so the brain does not have to come up with anything spontaneously. You can focus more on aspects of how you speak the script and not be concerned about having to process another speaker's comments and react to them.

There's a continuum of voice control for Sarah, with three main elements, which looks a bit like Figure 7.

Sarah vividly recalls some comments she had about her voice when she was starting out in radio. In her first job as a presenter, her boss told her that he could not let her on air until she sounded less miserable. 'It turns out that my natural voice is one of misery!' she says, with a wry smile. 'He said: "You need to speak with a smile in your voice." Ever since then, as a presenter,

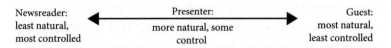

| Newsreader:
least natural,
most controlled | Presenter:
more natural, some
control | Guest:
most natural,
least controlled |

Figure 7 Sarah Walker's continuum of voice control

I've always done that. I can't imagine it's not had an impact on the way I speak when I'm off air.' I don't think she reads the news in a miserable way, either, but it may be less appropriate to speak with a smile.

Sarah has also had lots of positive comments about her voice, particularly to do with how calm and reassuring it sounds. 'I remember someone saying that I had a voice that you'd want to be stuck in a lift with. Somehow reassuring. And calming.' She confesses that another former boss suggested she work hard at being quite calm, mostly because 'women in particular don't like listening to women'. A calm, reassuring voice can help counteract that. I venture that people gravitate towards radio voices which have this quality, and it seems that Sarah's has this—as does Darren Redick's. Sarah explains that one strategy is to sit down when she's presenting rather than to stand up, as standing up makes her speak more loudly and sound more excited. 'I discovered that sitting down would calm me down completely.' Stress affects the voice, whether it's mental or physical, and that includes differences in posture. This reminds me of what Andrea was saying about how getting the voice right in a tribute act is as much about posture as the voice itself.

Sarah is yet another person who does not like the sound of her own voice. But it's clear that other people really do. After a bit of probing and a (very British) reluctance to sing her own praises, she tells me that she's been told she is one of the best newsreaders people have heard, and that people love the clarity of her voice. Her best compliment, aside from me saying her voice sounded chocolaty? 'That's right up there!' she says. 'One of my old bosses told me: "Your voice sings out of the radio to me in the morning". I remember her saying that.'

The voice and accent coach

I mentioned earlier in the book that Margaret Thatcher, once referred to as 'shrill', altered her speaking voice, and that this had probably had a direct impact on her selection as leader of the Conservative party and subsequent elevation to Prime Minister.

There are people who change the way they use their voice to fit in with different social or work situations. In fact, almost everyone does this to some extent. Some people, as we have seen in this chapter, might do this consciously or subconsciously when in some kind of performance context. And then there are the people who train others to understand their voices so they can deliberately change the way they speak for personal or professional reasons.

Mary is a London-based professional accent coach, originally from Northampton. She trains performing arts students at LAMDA (the London Academy of Music and Dramatic Arts) and coaches working actors one to one—some rather famous— to understand how to use their voices differently for different acting roles and scenarios. This includes being able to consciously manipulate things like accent, pitch, loudness, tempo, and voice quality to reflect different personality types, power hierarchies, emotions, and general states of being, physical and mental.

She has also been indispensable to me when I have needed someone to provide recordings of speech for students to use as stimuli in dissertation experiments. For example, one student wanted to look at how voice quality and accent contributed to the success of different kinds of food advertisements. Think the Marks and Spencer ones for chocolate fondant puddings, with a sexy-sounding female voice, low in pitch and breathy, describing how the chocolate sauce oozes out when you insert your spoon...Oh boy, I want a chocolate fondant NOW! Or the up-tempo, matter-of-fact frozen food store ones, high in average pitch and wide in pitch range, explaining that 'mums go to Iceland' to buy easy-cook food so they can fit everything into their busy day and still look like domestic goddesses. Interesting how food advertisements are often voiced by female actors.

There was music on the advertisements my student wanted to use. We didn't want that to have a bearing on how the advertisements were perceived, and we couldn't work out a way of removing the music without compromising the speech. Mary very kindly reproduced all the speech in the advertisements, effectively mimicking the voices. The student could hardly believe how similar Mary's versions sounded. It's nice to have friends with superb talents who don't mind sharing them.

We start by talking about the voice and accent actors working in the UK are going to need most often—and that's an RP-type accent. Acting students doing degrees usually start off with this in their first and second years. This accent is associated with a deep, resonant voice in the acting profession, and people from different regions of the UK and different parts of the world have to be taught how to produce the accent with this deep, resonant voice. She says some practitioners refer to it as 'true voice', a term Mary disputes, as she personally feels voice is bound up with identity, and a person's true voice will depend on who they are, not on a drama school construct. Whether this is the case or not, acting students are trained to be able to produce a deep, resonant, RP-like accent because that's most often what some parts of the industry want—and what the audience expects. Being unable to do so may hinder a British-based actor's progress. The other accent they will need—sometimes more than the RP-one—is some kind of General American, north Mid-Western rhotic accent.

If you'd like to hear someone go from a North American accent to a British one in three minutes, describing what he's doing as he goes, listen to Professor David Ley. He makes doing accents look like a piece of cake.

Scan here or go to https://www.youtube.com/ watch?v=IdAKIzq7bvs to hear Professor David Ley on the British accent

In the third year of study, student actors will often find they are playing parts involving regional accents. That's Mary's speciality. This ranges from Cockney to Afro-Caribbean to—well, almost anything. 'We can be doing *The Pitman Painters* and everyone has to sound like a Geordie collier.' Mary uses a range of techniques, including reference to the International Phonetic Alphabet and the industry's own way of describing voice quality, and explains how 'the intonation stuff is hugely important for getting the accent to absolutely land.'

Mary's journey into accent coaching is not dissimilar to Ian Danter's entry into radio presenting; it involved her ability to speak with various accents. She started off working in theatre in Birmingham, doing lighting and stage management. She then did a couple of small acting jobs—including one which involved being eight different characters throughout the play, each with a different accent—before deciding that she was enjoying the accents but not the acting so much. 'It was interesting how I was treated as an actor. Totally different to when I was dressed in black being a techie.' I get the strong impression being the actor was the negative experience. 'Acting wasn't for me,' she says. Being an accent coach means she still gets to enjoy doing the accents, but doesn't have to wait for someone to choose her for an acting part because she looks right on stage. Win-win.

She describes her own voice as deep, variable, and explains that she consciously uses a range of accent features, drawing from places she's lived and accents she's currently teaching. She does this for two main reasons: to provide some balance to the high proportion of RP-speaking colleagues; and because she wants to show the RP-accent is one of many students can put on, like a hat—a bit like my sun hat versus horse riding helmet analogy. 'There are cases of students going home and people saying "Why are you talking like that?" because their voices have changed,' she says. 'It can be a bit tricky for the students from a social perspective if they can't still do their own regional accent. They probably haven't realized there's been a change. People can get offended.' She explains she's known as 'the posh one' among her family in Northampton, and feels quite distant from them. This might be why she is keen for students to be able to understand what they're doing with their voices and accent, so that they can change it and not get stuck with something that doesn't represent them.

When Mary is training a specific accent—and this can last for a whole term in the case of students—she teaches the class in that accent. She explains that this has a tangible effect on the way she is perceived because accents are aligned so much with personality. 'If students have heard me using an American accent for the whole term, and then at the end of term I drop into my British accent to explain what we're doing next term, their reaction is like you've produced flowers out of nowhere—like a magic trick. They forget you're British.

'But if someone asks me "What is your own accent?" I have to say I don't know any more. There are so many bits from so many different parts of my life, including teaching. Things stick because I do them so often.'

Mary deliberately changes her voice to sound more feminine when she's on the telephone: 'I go brighter, lighter, a bit breathy. The voice I'm using now wouldn't be my phone voice.' This may be because she perceives her usual voice to be relatively low in pitch, but I also wonder whether the 'acting' telephone voice is like this and she's picked it up. Mary also changes her accent to achieve more favourable reactions in situations such as meetings: 'I've had to kind of RP-up because I felt I wasn't being taken seriously'. She even suggests using a more RP-like accent can help in part to balance out gender inequalities. 'The really sad thing is: it works. I am taken more seriously with that accent.' BBC presenter Steph McGovern's comments on this topic reinforce Mary's viewpoint. I wonder how much the accent she's using with me as we chat is an artefact of having me as an interlocutor.

What about social occasions? 'I've been in situations when I've been so bored, I've done an accent all evening,' says Mary, laughing. How does this affect people? 'Not much, unless I've dropped it at the end. Then they can look a bit shocked if they think I'm "the Scottish person" or something. But if I've gone in with an accent and people have totally accepted it, then it shows I've got it right. Particularly if it's with that specific accent group.

'But if I tell people I'm an accent coach, it just turns into "accent jukebox"—"Can you do this accent? Can you do that accent?"—so I tend to say I'm a teacher.' She really doesn't like performing to order.

Mary believes that there's still a lot of accent prejudice in some areas of acting. 'If you go in for an audition with a strong regional accent, you're going to have a problem,' she says. 'You'll be told to get rid of it.' Students need to be aware of this and be prepared to use RP or General American at minimum, unless they are asked for a specific accent. She also mentions how actors from BAME backgrounds—standing for 'Black, Asian, and Minority Ethnic'—are expected to be able to do accents associated with those groups, as they are likely to be cast that way. 'We have to get them to think about the accents they're going to be asked to do in the profession. If you're a black actor and you can't do some kind of Caribbean or Multicultural London English accent, for example, you need to learn it.'

I sense a degree of sadness in Mary when she talks about having her first session with student actors, listening to their accents and knowing that anyone with a reasonably strong accent or 'high, thin voice' is going to have that 'beaten out of them' in favour of the low, resonant RP-type accent and General American. 'Your accent is you. How is that not acceptable?' she says. But she admits that, if people choose to go into the acting profession, they have to take this on board. 'There's a very narrow view of what an acceptable accent is, and I'd love to change that...but in a drama school, you've got to reflect what's in the industry.' She goes on to explain how Liverpool, Scouse, and Manchester accents are associated with 'canny' or 'cheeky' characters, whereas 'funny' characters often have Birmingham, Irish, or Yorkshire accents. If you've got one of those accents and don't or can't change it, you may either be typecast or out of a job.

Such is the pervasive strength of stereotypes. If what we see on stage and screen is a reflection of our stereotypes, it is just going to exacerbate the situation. It's good to hear a greater number of television continuity announcers with accents that reflect regional or ethnic differences, and to see people with different accents presenting on national television. But if playwrights are still writing to stereotypes, and professional voices are expected to reflect that, we've got a long way to go.

Professional voices, particularly those in the media, are often very distinctive, and recognized by a lot of people. We hear this or that person on the radio, television, or online and we are in little or no doubt about who they are before we see them. We build up a mental image based on how the person's voice sounds.

If we hear an impression of someone, it can be difficult at first to know if it's the actual speaker or the impressionist, because what the impressionist does (as Ian Danter explained) is find those things that are particularly distinctive about the way a person speaks, and use those distinctive cues to give an 'impression' of the voice. This can sometimes be quite convincing and—in the case of professional impressionists like Tracey Ullman and Rory Bremner—used for comedic effect.

There are instances, however, when distinctive patterns of a person's voice are used for a very different purpose: to catch a criminal. This is the topic of Chapter 5.

CHAPTER 5

Your voice is your witness
Forensic speaker analysis in criminal investigations

F aith Mbanefo[1] works as Operations Manager in a community centre in a culturally diverse region of the UK. Among other things, the community centre runs a crèche for the under-fives, martial arts and music training for school-aged children, English language classes for people from non-English-speaking communities in the area, women's development groups for women from different cultures, support groups for the over-fifties, and lots of community volunteering activities.

Early one Monday morning, Faith arrives at the community centre. She's the only one there and, while she has quite a hectic home life and values the early morning time to herself, she does find it a bit lonely until other people start to arrive.

She starts checking the voicemail messages left over the weekend. There are the usual ones asking if this or that class is running, whether there are places at the crèche, and to find out how much it is to hire the main hall for a Saturday sometime next year. Faith waits, pen poised, for each message, writing down the contact details of the callers and noting their requests or requirements. But one message causes her to press the stop button almost immediately that she realizes what is going on.

It's a racial hate message.

The language in the message is so distressing that Faith sits with her hand over her mouth for a short period of time, breathing deeply to calm herself down. She then irrationally runs to the window and looks out as if the person who made the call might be standing there ready to cause trouble; she feels threatened, not just for herself but also for the people who come to the centre. She's just beginning to wish someone else was there with her when Jo, who runs the crèche, arrives and calls 'Good morning!', passing the reception hatch. She then comes back again when she realizes Faith did not give her usual cheery response. Faith explains what she has just heard and, after Jo has made her a cup of tea, the two gingerly replay the voicemail message.

Initially, they decide it's probably just a one-off—some drunk idiot ringing up as a dare—and decide not to do anything about it or mention it to anyone. However, Faith saves the recording and notes the date and time, just in case, even though she wants to delete it immediately.

Two weeks later, the same thing happens. This time, Faith tells the centre Director, who rings the police.

The police investigation finds that the calls have been made from one of the few public phone boxes in the area. While it does not directly point at the phone box, footage from a CCTV camera identifies a couple of suspects who fit the general profile and were in that area at the times the calls were made. They are brought in for questioning. The suspects deny the charge, one claiming that he has no problem with people from different racial backgrounds . . . but, when pressed, does admit he is not keen on the number of asylum seekers who have been housed around there recently, many of whom are attending English language classes at the centre. He perceives them to be a drain on resources that should be going to 'local' people. The police, however, do not have enough to go on and so look for other types of evidence. One of those types of evidence is arrived at through forensic speaker comparison.

Forensic speaker comparison: what's involved?

Forensic speaker comparison uses auditory and acoustic analysis techniques to 'catch criminals'.

I have been involved in forensic speaker comparison since 2002. When I was initially approached by a police force to do this kind of work, while I knew I had the required skills, I had no experience in the area, and so worked with a colleague who had had a lot of experience to learn the craft. You can now do a postgraduate qualification in forensic speech science—for example, there's one offered at the University of York (UK),[2] which is taught by experienced phoneticians and forensic practitioners.

Forensic speaker comparison involves taking a minimum of two recordings and subjecting them to auditory and acoustic analysis to determine how likely it is that they were spoken by the same person. One or more recordings will usually have been made by the police at the time of interview; this is known as the 'reference' sample. These can be made on a number of media but, at the time of writing, some police forces still use audio cassette. The other recording(s)—known as the 'disputed' sample—could also be recorded on to a number of different devices, but are very often telephone recordings. In instances where a suspect has committed fraud by, for example, pretending to be someone else over a phone banking line, the recording is usually available from the bank; you've probably stopped noticing the customer service announcement at the start telling you the call will be recorded.

If it's a voicemail message, it could be stored on some kind of hard-disk drive, in flash format, or on microcassette if it's a really old machine. My voicemail at work sends me a recording in MP3 format via email to make sure I haven't missed any messages.

While a certain amount of acoustic examination can be carried out by anyone who knows their way around computer speech software, auditory analysis is something which requires years of specialist training. The law also requires that forensic phoneticians work in groups so that our analysis can be checked by at least one other suitably trained colleague; this helps the analysis stand up better in court, should it come to that.

Before a forensic phonetician can even start this analysis, however, two conditions have to be satisfied: there has to be a large enough quantity of both samples to make comparison possible, and the samples have to be of good enough quality. Among other things, the forensic phonetician will be looking for distinctive features of the speaker's speech which are similar in both samples, and so needs a range of language to work with; if a speaker simply says 'No comment' all the way through the police interview, there's not much scope for comparison!

I should make clear at this point that, while it is possible to rule out that the two recordings come from the same speaker, we can't ever arrive at a definite positive result. 'Extremely strong support' for the two recordings being from the same person is the closest a forensic phonetician can ever come to being certain. Although each person has distinctive features in his or her speech, your voice is not the same as a fingerprint. If I were to say the same word or phrase over and over again, even though I have been trained to produce nearly identical dictation passages for students, there would still be differences in my production, some of which can be picked up by ear. The acoustic signal would certainly be different.

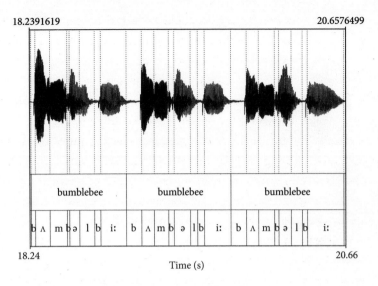

18.2391619   20.6576499

| bumblebee | bumblebee | bumblebee |

| b | ʌ | m | b | ə | l | b | iː | b | ʌ | m | b | ə | l | b | iː | b | ʌ | m | b | ə | l | b | iː |

18.24   20.66

Time (s)

Figure 8   *Bumblebee* x 3

Figure 8 is a computer display of the waveform of me saying the word *bumblebee* three times over with the same intonation pattern.

So, what information are we seeing here, exactly?

The top tier, looking like a series of different-sized fuzzy blobs, is the waveform. Underneath that is a tier showing you where the three words begin and end, and another one showing where each of the sounds are in the stream of speech—this is also reflected in the waveform above (for selected sound files, see the companion site).

The waveform shows you how loud a speaker has produced certain sounds in comparison with others. It also shows some other features of sounds, such as whether the vocal folds are vibrating. If they are not, the image is more like a thin horizontal line. The word *bumblebee* has all voiced sounds, but in English /b/ sounds tend not to be fully voiced, and (as described in Chapter 1) you have to stop the air to produce a /b/ as it is a

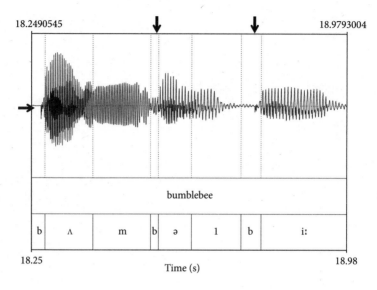

18.2490545   18.9793004

bumblebee

| b | ʌ | m | b | ə | 1 | b | iː |

18.25   18.98

Time (s)

Figure 9   *Bumblebee* No. 1, /b/ sounds highlighted with arrows

plosive sound, so you can see there is less energy where I'm saying /b/ than for the other sounds (see Figure 9, showing one *bumblebee*, where the /b/ sounds are indicated with arrows).

In Figure 9, you can also see that the waveform is made up of a series of what looks like regular vertical lines. Each of these lines is basically one vibration of the vocal folds—1 Hz. For every voiced sound, there will be several of these, depending on the speaker. When we say for female speakers we expect the average to be 200–250 Hz, for example, that means we'd expect there to be 200–250 of these vertical lines per second. We're seeing just under three quarters of a second in Figure 9. When we have regular vertical lines like this, we say the waveform is periodic.

For voiceless sounds, the display will not show the same regular pattern, as the vocal folds are not in vibration. We'll get to some voiceless sounds later.

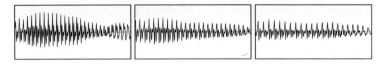

Figure 10　The waveforms of the three STRUT vowels in *bumblebee* x 3

Going back to Figure 8, you can see the pattern for each word is similar, but not identical. For example, the first vowel of the first syllable of *bumblebee* is much darker in the first word than in the others, and the vowel in the last syllable is much longer in the third version than in the others.

If we zoom in on the waveforms of the first vowel in each word—the STRUT vowel—we can also see they are not identical (Figure 10). Even if I think I'm saying the words over and over again in exactly the same way, the acoustic information will show that, physically, that is just not possible.

So, what is involved in forensic speaker comparison? There are two main components: auditory analysis and acoustic analysis.

Auditory analysis

As you will have gathered from previous chapters in this book, your voice can reveal a lot about you. It can tell people where you are from, in some cases narrowing it down to a very local region; it can give away your level of education, your social group and aspirations, your age, your gender, your ethnicity, and all sorts of other personal information about you.

The auditory analysis carried out in forensic speaker comparison takes both top-down (starting with the bigger picture) and bottom-up (looking at minute detail) approaches in order to give a full and thorough analysis of distinctive speaker patterns.

The forensic phonetician sits down with the material and listens to it over and over again in order to make a written account of the features of speech.

Top-down information will include whether a speaker uses particular pause fillers such as 'um', 'er', or 'eh', discourse markers such as 'd'you know what I mean', 'like', and 'innit', terms of address such as 'love, 'mate', 'me duck', and so on, or particular keywords and phrases. Many of these are regional, age specific, or linked to some other social group, but some are idiolectal, i.e. specific to a particular person. For example, many younger speakers in London using the accent known as Multicultural London English (MLE) end phrases with 'innit'. While this would be noted in the analysis, it is rather commonplace, and so might not be particularly helpful unless the speaker in the disputed sample did it all the time and the one in the reference sample systematically used something else or did not use it at all.

The analysis will also consider patterns of intonation. As we have seen earlier in this book, many English speakers now use something known as uptalk, which involves a rise in intonation on statements where one would expect to hear a fall—but not all speakers do this. There are also regionally specific patterns of intonation. Northern Irish intonation sounds quite different from intonation in the speech of someone from the very south of the Republic of Ireland, for example, and so this might be a useful clue to whether the speech in the two samples is likely to have come from one and the same speaker or two different ones.

Voice quality is also a feature which might be important here; is the voice creaky, or breathy, or particularly nasal-sounding? For example, the speech of actors Joanna Lumley (although not when she's playing Patsy in TV sitcom *Absolutely Fabulous*) and Marilyn Monroe sounds quite breathy, a feature often associated with sexy female voices, as noted in Chapter 3. If a male speaker's voice sounded breathy, it would be quite distinctive. As we also saw in Chapter 3, creaky voice is associated with older male speakers of Received Pronunciation, but it can also be heard near the very end of an utterance when a speaker is tired or physiologically running out of air, as the vocal folds vibrate much less rapidly and the pitch sounds very low under these circumstances. Also in Chapter 3, we observed how creaky voice is now a pattern heard among younger female speakers in some populations; it's increasingly found among younger men too. If the voice is creaky for longer than just at the very end of an utterance, it might be distinctive enough to attract the forensic phonetician's attention, and will certainly be noted.

Something else which might have a bearing is the environment in which a recording was made. This is less interesting in the reference sample, as we know who the speaker in this sample is, and the recording will usually have been made in a police interview room. For the disputed sample, however, background noise can be useful in the analysis and rather telling. If a suspect is thought to have made a phone call from a particular location, for example, evidence of this location might be found on the recording. Are there specific church bells in the background, or the striking of a clock? Do any sirens in the background locate the call as coming from near the accident and emergency department of a hospital, a police station or fire station, or near an emergency incident? Is the television or radio on in the background, and what is being broadcast? Can any other voices be heard which might help identify the speaker? And so on.

Bottom-up information focuses on fine phonetic detail in a speaker's speech. Is the speaker pronouncing consonants or vowels in a distinctive way? Of course, the speech of all speakers is distinctive to some extent, but here we are looking for anything which particularly stands out as being unusual.

Some speakers have a 'whistly' /s/ sound, for example. This is not dependent on regional or social accent. For famous speakers with this speech feature, listen to recordings or video footage of Sir Patrick Stewart (*Star Trek*'s Captain Jean-Luc Picard and the *X-Men* movie franchise's Professor X) or Sir Ian McKellen (Gandalf the Grey/White from the *Lord of the Rings/The Hobbit* movies and Magneto in *X-Men*), both of whom have the occasional whistled /s/, mainly at the ends of words. One thing which causes this to happen is when the speaker is making too small a gap between their tongue tip and alveolar ridge (the bumpy ridge behind the teeth) to the point that the friction needed for the /s/ sound is altered and the sound comes out as a whistle. It can also arise as a result of various dental procedures; an article in the *New York Times* discusses how cosmetic dentistry or the fitting of dentures can result in a whistled /s/ sound when the speaker did not have one prior to treatment, and admits that it can be very difficult for speakers to get rid of a whistled /s/.[3] While it may seem a far stretch to suggest that dental records might be used to identify the perpetrator of a crime (cannibalism, anyone?), this sort of information might be extremely valuable, and not just from the point of view of forensic speaker comparison.

In Chapter 4, I mentioned that speakers also vary a lot in the way they produce /r/ sounds. Again, this may not be dependent on regional or social accent. In British English, for example, the /r/ sound could be produced as a 'normal' /r/, which involves the tongue tip or body moving up and forwards in the oral cavity, usually with a lot of lip-rounding. Some people, however, produce a labiodental /r/, and another, more posh British English way of saying the sound (which is to do with social accent) is to produce it the way many Americans say /t/ sounds in words like *Betty* and *little*, which is known as a tap and is a bit like a very quick /d/ sound. My singing teacher in primary school, Mr Bird, used to insist we 'rolled' our /r/ sounds; the technical term for this is a trilled /r/, and is a feature of Spanish. There is also a difference between rhotic and non-rhotic accents—i.e. between those which produce an /r/ everywhere there is one in the spelling, and those which do not.

Think about your own /r/ sounds. Which of these variants I've just described do you use? Or do you pronounce it another way?

Vowel sounds can also be distinctive. As well as regional variation—e.g., how you say *bath* will depend on where you're from—use of particular social accents will have an impact on your vowel sounds. Speakers of Multicultural London English, for example, are not all necessarily from London, as the accent has a foothold in other large urban centres in the UK, such as Manchester (Multicultural Manchester English) and Birmingham (Multicultural Birmingham English). The MLE accent, and others associated with it, has vowels which sound more like those of Jamaican English.

Let's take the example of the vowel in words like *day* and *late* (the FACE vowel). In many other London-based accents, this vowel involves the tongue moving from a slightly open position in the mouth to a place where it is more close to the roof of the mouth. As we saw in Chapter 1, we call this type of vowel a diphthong. A vowel in which the tongue stays more or less in the same place is called a monophthong, an example for many English accents being the vowel in DRESS. In Multicultural London English, the vowel in FACE is a monophthong, i.e., the tongue does not move but stays in one place, and sounds a bit like a long DRESS vowel.

There are other accents of British English which have a monophthong for the FACE vowel, one being Yorkshire, but Manchester speakers notably do not. If a suspected criminal is from London or Manchester and displays features of MLE in their speech, this can help to identify which speech community a speaker belongs to, and narrow down the possibility of two samples being from different speakers.

Acoustic analysis

Once a comprehensive auditory analysis of both samples has been made, the forensic phonetician can then select aspects of the samples for acoustic analysis. This is done using speech analysis software such as free programs *Speech Filing System*[4] and *Praat*,[5] or Kay Elemetrics's commercial application and hardware *Computer Speech Lab* (CSL).[6] Aspects we often measure include fundamental frequency (spoken pitch), formant frequencies, and spectral information for any distinctive articulations of specific vowels or consonants. We are looking to see how similar each feature we measure in the disputed sample is in comparison with the speech in the reference sample.

Right at the start of this process, however, we often have to do something called filtering to the reference sample. This is because disputed material from a telephone call does not have the full spectrum of frequencies found in recordings made in police interview rooms. I used to get post addressed to 'Jane Fetter' if I'd given my name to someone over the phone without specifying 's for *sugar*' or similar. The sounds /f/ and /s/ can sound quite similar on the phone because the higher frequencies produced when I say /s/ are missing in a telephone call, but the lower frequencies in /s/ overlap with those in /f/.

As you know, animals such as dogs can hear a wide spectrum of sounds which humans cannot, and human voices tend to be spoken within the range of frequencies that humans can perceive. Human speech sounds range in frequency from around 80 Hz to 14 kHz, although frequencies above 5 kHz really are exceptional, and it is not common for speakers to use the whole of that range. To recap, the average male voice is around 100–150 Hz, average female voices are around double that at 200–300 Hz, and children's voices are on average around 300–400 Hz. Telephone calls are usually limited to a range of 300 Hz to 3.4 kHz—although HD voice, also known as wideband audio, used by many smartphone networks, extends from 50 Hz to around 7 kHz.

As you can imagine, the non-HD frequency range is going to put a limit on what forensic phoneticians can measure. The good news is that speech is a very complex mixture of frequencies and that not all information is based on the basic spoken pitch range of the voice. Computer speech analysis programmes have filters built into them which mimic the effect of telephone filters, and so it is relatively easy to apply a filter to the reference sample, as required. We will then usually measure spoken pitch range in the two samples for comparison, along with the average (or mean), and the trend (or mode). The trend is usually more interesting than the average, as it shows the frequency around which the speaker's pitch clusters, and so can be a more accurate indicator of the perceived 'general' pitch of a speaker's voice than the average.

We then look at vowels and consonant sounds, particularly where auditory analysis has picked up an interesting pattern. For vowels, we measure and compare acoustic properties known as formants using a spectrographic display (the spectrogram) built into the speech analysis software.

While there are similarities in the shape of the inside of the mouth across human beings, each person's oral cavity is shaped slightly differently, and this will have an effect on the way speech is produced and how it sounds. A formant is a measurable acoustic resonance in the vocal tract, and each vowel sound has a number of these resonances which will be in a distinctive pattern for a given population of speakers and also for individuals.

You can see an example of spectrographic displays (or spectrograms) showing formants for the vowels in FLEECE, BATH, and PRICE spoken by me in Figures 11, 12, and 13 (for colour images where the formants are clearer, see the companion website at

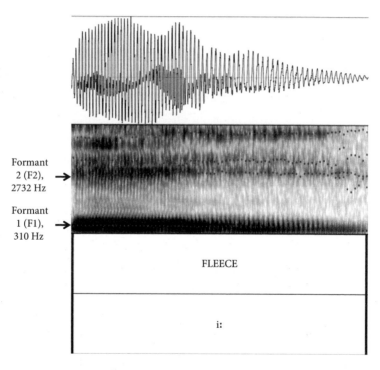

Figure 11   The FLEECE vowel, /iː/

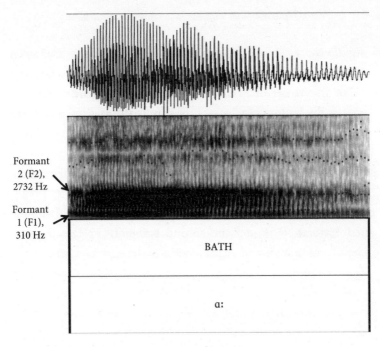

Figure 12   The BATH vowel, /ɑː/

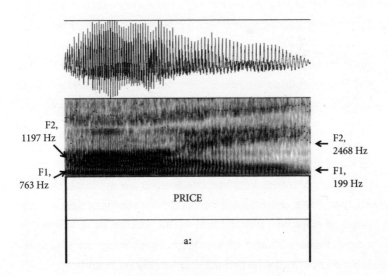

Figure 13   The PRICE vowel, /aɪ/

http://www.oup.co.uk/companion/setter). The formants are shown in the tier under the waveform and are fuzzy-looking black bands.

For the vowel in FLEECE, the first two formants—the one nearest the bottom (Formant 1, or simply F1) and the one above it (Formant 2, or F2)—are far apart.

In BATH, they are much closer together.

In PRICE, they start close together and then move apart as the tongue moves upwards in the oral cavity (try it).

In the study of accents, we usually measure and report on the first formant (F1) and the second formant (F2) in order to identify how a person is producing a vowel sound and which social group they might belong to. F1 has the lowest frequency, appearing as the lowest band in the diagrams above, and corresponds more or less to how high the tongue is in the mouth; if the tongue is high in the mouth, the frequency in Hz is low (averaging around 319 Hz for female speakers in the word FLEECE), and if the tongue is low in the mouth, the frequency is higher (averaging around 779 Hz for BATH—mine starts a bit lower than that but then moves up). F2, which is the next band up, corresponds more or less to whether the tongue is towards the front or back of the oral cavity; if the tongue is forward, the frequency is high (around 2723 Hz for a female speaker's FLEECE vowel, on average), and if the tongue is back, it is lower (around 1181 Hz for BATH).[7] We may also want to measure F3 and F4, but this will depend on how much detail we need and what sort of sounds we are looking at.

As far as consonants are concerned, we are again looking for distinctive patterns which occur in both the reference and disputed samples. Going back to the notion of a whistly /s/ sound, Figures 14 and 15 are diagrams showing me saying the word *seesaw* with whistly and non-whistly /s/ sounds.

You can see that, although the /s/ sounds have a similar pattern looking a bit like a raincloud at the top of the formant display, the whistled /s/ in Figure 14 is different from the normal /s/ in Figure 15

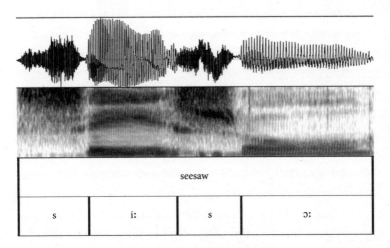

	seesaw		
s	iː	s	ɔː

Figure 14   Whistly /s/ *seesaw*

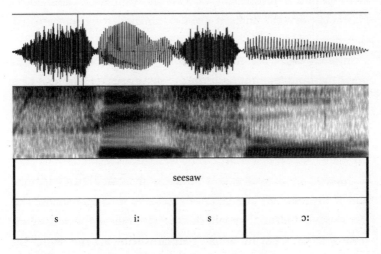

	seesaw		
s	iː	s	ɔː

Figure 15   Non-whistly /s/ *seesaw*

both on the waveform (top tier) and the spectrogram (next tier down). The 'raincloud' area is aperiodic, so it looks like a bit of a mess in comparison with the vowels, which have a clearly defined periodic pattern. /s/ sounds are voiceless fricatives which make a lot of noise but have no vocal fold vibration, so we expect to see a large 'blob' on the waveform for the /s/. Although it is quite a subtle difference, the aperiodic noise in the spectrogram area of the whistled /s/ in Figure 14 has a wider pattern of distribution than in the non-whistled /s/ in Figure 15. If this was a feature of the speech in the disputed sample, we would compare this information with that appearing in the reference sample to see if there were any similarities. This would be repeated with other distinctive features to build up a picture of the speech in both samples so a report could be made to the police.

But remember: we cannot state categorically that the two speakers are one and the same. We can only say how well the speech from the two samples matches, using evidence from the auditory and acoustic analysis, with the strongest recommendation being that the analysis gives extremely strong support that they were produced by the same speaker.

In many cases, presenting evidence to the suspect which supports the samples coming from the same speaker can lead to a confession, particularly if the suspect's defence lawyer has also hired a forensic phonetician who reaches more or less the same conclusion. But, in some instances, the evidence from my team is presented as part of a court case, which means that one of us may be asked to speak as an expert witness at the trial. If that happens, and if the case for the defence disagrees with our analysis of the spoken evidence, we will have to face one of our colleagues from another team in court... which can be a nerve-wracking experience.

Voice parades and earwitnesses

Student Dan Matthews is on his way back to his university hall of residence one afternoon when he hears some people shouting in the alleyway a little way up the road. He can't see what's going on as the fence is too high on his side, but whatever it is doesn't sound very good. He hears what he thinks is an adult female voice almost screaming at the other person: 'Gimme your phone! Give it me or you'll be for it!' The other person sounds like a child, frightened and crying.

Dan decides to see if he can help, and speeds up to a run. By the time he gets there, only the child is left in the alleyway, his bag lying open on the floor with schoolbooks, a lunch box, and other belongings strewn across the path. He looks about eleven or twelve years old.

Dan ascertains that the boy isn't too badly hurt, and that he has had his new phone stolen by a woman he hadn't seen before. Dan calls the police. He asks the boy where the woman went, but the boy isn't sure, and Dan can't hear anyone running away so he decides not to give chase. The area is rather built up so the woman could have gone anywhere.

Dan asks the boy what the woman looked like. He says she had a blue hoodie on with the hood pulled right over, and it was zipped up so high that the front almost covered her mouth. He couldn't really see her face. He's too upset to want to say much else.

Dan calls the boy's parents and stays with him until the police and parents arrive. He's asked if he will give a witness statement and agrees, but tells the police he didn't see the woman, only heard her shouting. When he gives his statement, he recounts what he heard the assailant say and how she said it. The police say they will be in touch. He is later called in to be an earwitness in a voice parade.

A voice parade, or voice line-up, is a bit like the standard identity parade, but for voices. In an identity parade, a witness is presented with a row of similar-looking people fitting the physical appearance of the suspect—one of which is the suspect—and has to point out the one they thought they saw at the scene of the crime. In a voice parade, a witness who has said they heard the suspect speaking or shouting at the scene, but didn't see them and doesn't know who they are, is presented with a series of speech samples and has to decide whether the voice they heard is present among the samples.

Forensic phoneticians Toby Hudson, Kirsty McDougall, and Vincent Hughes[8] explain that the history of the earwitness in court cases goes back as far as 1660, although in the 1660 case the witness simply said they recognized the suspect's voice. There was no attempt at offering the witness other voices to see how reliable that evidence was.

Hudson and colleagues point out that, even in very well-constructed voice parades, identification by earwitnesses is often not very good, meaning the evidence is not very useful. But there is a huge amount of variation. All kinds of factors can affect how good recall is, including how long the earwitness was exposed to the voice, if they have made a concerted effort to remember the voice—particularly if they realized a crime was being committed at the time—and whether they come from the same local speech community. There has also been some research suggesting blind listeners are better in voice line-ups than sighted ones, presumably because their sense of hearing is heightened...but there is other evidence suggesting blind listeners do not have an advantage.

Another issue is whether the earwitness knows (or thinks they know) who the speaker is: a family member, a friend, a regular acquaintance—or even a celebrity. In this case, rather than presenting the earwitness with a range of samples and asking them to say whether the voice they heard is present, forensic speech expert Francis Nolan recommends that they should be asked whether any of the voices belongs to the person they know. This might not look that much different, but it tests the witness's familiarity with a specific voice and how reliable that is. I know people who have mixed up family members on the phone, sometimes with hilarious consequences. They've been so certain that they are speaking to, say, the daughter rather than the mother that they have given some pretty sensitive information away to the wrong person!

So, how is a voice parade put together? Where do the other voices come from? Hudson and colleagues describe the process.

In England and Wales, there are clear Home Office guidelines which state how voice parades should be constructed. All voices are from police interviews, and include a sample from the suspect and others from unrelated cases in which the speakers are similar in age, ethnicity, and regional and social background to the suspect. These other voices are known as 'foils'. There is a very careful selection process from twenty possible foils, which the forensic phonetician whittles down to eleven or twelve similar-sounding voices, based largely on how they sound, not using acoustic measurement. These are then further whittled down to eight foil voices by playing the voices to a group of naïve listeners—that is, listeners with no phonetic training—who make judgements about how similar the voices are.

As you can see, it is not just a matter of picking eight voices at random from the police database.

The earwitness will be presented with one-minute recordings from each of the nine speakers. These recordings are edited from the police interviews to remove anything specifically related to the crime. But Hudson and colleagues tell us that there is yet another step which has to take place before the recordings can be presented to the earwitness.

To avoid the possibility that the target speaker 'sounds like a criminal'—or more like a criminal than the foils—naïve listeners are again called upon to make a judgement about how likely it is that each of the nine voices has committed a crime. This is called 'stereotype bias'.

We have seen elsewhere in this book how much listeners judge your personality and other factors just from the way you speak. Some speakers may therefore sound more guilty than others, based on their speech characteristics. If the naïve listeners rate all speakers in the sample as having more or less the same level of stereotype bias, it's OK to go ahead and use the recordings for the voice parade.

Phew!

As an earwitness, you only hear the recordings in the end product. The care which is taken to put together voice parades is testament to the diligence of the legal system in seeking to get a fair outcome for the suspect. But even then, when voice parade evidence is presented in court, it must be made clear by the expert presenting it that this is not an exact science and that misidentifications can be made.

Speaker profiling: Jihadi John and the Yorkshire Ripper

In August 2014, a terrorist known as 'Jihadi John' appeared in a video uploaded to YouTube performing the public execution of the US journalist, James Foley. After a lengthy speech in favour of his cause and against the West, he beheaded Foley. While the beheading itself was not shown, the severed head of the journalist appeared at the end of the video. He went on to film and post the execution of a number of American, British, Japanese, and Syrian nationals up until January 2015. The videos became increasingly gory, and the beheading of one Syrian victim was actually shown. It was a horrific series of events.

After the first video was posted in August 2014, an investigation immediately started to try to identify Jihadi John. But there wasn't much to go on. He was dressed completely in black, his head and face covered, with only his eyes visible through a very thin gap in the fabric. The films would have made it possible to work out his height and build. Other than that, he could be anyone.

But we did have a voice.

The UK media were very interested in this voice, as the accent had been identified as 'British'. That being the case, various UK phoneticians were asked to give their opinion to the media on where this man could be from, based on his speech. I was one of those phoneticians.

This is not the first time the voice of a killer has caused a media storm. In 1979, Assistant Chief Constable George Oldfield of the West Yorkshire Police was sent a cassette with a recording of someone purporting to be the Yorkshire Ripper. The Yorkshire Ripper murdered thirteen women in total in Yorkshire between 1975 and 1980, and attempted to murder seven others; the police had been trying to capture him, but his arrest had eluded them.

West Yorkshire police received the recording after they and *The Daily Mirror* newspaper had been sent three taunting letters over the course of 1978 and 1979, all claiming to be from the Yorkshire Ripper.

This was the message on the tape:

I'm Jack. I see you are having no luck catching me. I have the greatest respect for you, George, but Lord! You are no nearer catching me now than four years ago when I started. I reckon your boys are letting you down, George. They can't be much good, can they?

Evidence in the case had so far pointed strongly to the Ripper being from West Yorkshire. The voice in the recording, however, did not have a West Yorkshire accent.

West Yorkshire police recruited the respected phonetician and dialectician Stanley Ellis to help identify the speaker in the recording. After examining the recording, Ellis came to the conclusion that the speaker was from Castletown in Sunderland.

Ellis and other forensic experts warned the police that the recording might be a fake, but the conclusion that the Ripper might be from Castletown caused them to divert their efforts way from West Yorkshire to a search in that area of Sunderland. It was not until the real perpetrator, Peter Sutcliffe, confessed to the murders in 1981—claiming diminished responsibility on the basis of paranoid schizophrenia—that West Yorkshire Police accepted the recording and the letters had all been part of an elaborate hoax. On the day he was captured, Sutcliffe was in a car with another woman, apparently on their way to a gruesome end.

In the recording, the speaker referred to himself as 'Jack'. He later came to be known as 'Wearside Jack'; the river Wear flows through Sunderland, where it meets the sea. But his actual identity was not uncovered until much later than Sutcliffe's arrest and conviction.

In 2005—over twenty years after the original investigation— the evidence from the hoax was reviewed using modern forensic techniques to test the DNA left from the saliva on the gummed seal of one of the envelopes of the letters sent to West Yorkshire police. A match was found with DNA taken from a man called John Humble, following his arrest for another misdemeanour in 2000. He was called in for questioning. Humble told the police during their interviews that he had attended a school in Castletown—the area of Newcastle where Wearside Jack was from. Humble said he had watched, nervously, as his neighbours had been interviewed by the police about the Ripper in the latter stages of the original investigation. He himself had escaped interview.

Humble was later sentenced to eight years in jail for perverting the course of justice. Ellis's evidence, that the speaker on the tape had come from the Castletown area of Sunderland, eventually aided in this conviction. If it hadn't been for Wearside Jack's recording, Humble might well not have been found guilty of the hoax which misled the search for the Yorkshire Ripper, giving Sutcliffe time to murder an additional three women before he was finally captured.

Let's go back to Jihadi John.

My involvement with the Jihadi John case was purely to give the media an opinion on anything I could glean about the terrorist and executioner from his voice and accent. The first thing I pointed out was that, as we could not see his lips move because of the face covering, the video footage might have a voiceover coming from another speaker. This could make the speaker some kind of accessory but, if the speaker was not the person in the video executing Foley, it put a different angle on what was going on.

Having said that, I was able to tell a number of things from Jihadi John's voice.

First, his accent. This was an accent known as Multicultural London English, or MLE.

I've talked about this accent earlier in this chapter. Here's a little more clarification. It is thought to have originated in the northeast London borough of Hackney, and has pronunciation aspects from, mainly, Afro-Caribbean English, South Asian English, Greek English, and London English. So, definitely a British accent. But there was more that I could say about him from the way that he spoke.

For a start, the language he was using in the video was eloquent, if chilling. This gave me the impression that he was probably educated to university level.

I was also asked whether I thought he was an immigrant. Based on the way he spoke, I suggested that—if he was an immigrant—he had come to Britain as a young child. While it is not impossible to sound like a native speaker of a variety of English (or any language) if you learn it at a later age, it is very difficult once you get to puberty. There are lots of theories about why this might be the case, including suggestions that the brain goes through a process called lateralization at some point and this affects the ability to learn language effectively after the age of twelve to thirteen. Whatever the case, evidence from people learning languages all over the world has shown that, once people hit those teenage years, it is difficult to pronounce a new language like a native speaker. As Jihadi John was using the MLE accent with no signs of interference from the speech patterns of another language, I thought it unlikely that he had entered the UK as an older child or adolescent. That's if he was an immigrant.

I was not involved in the investigation by the authorities. Those of us who had been asked to comment by the media waited for the authorities to conclude their investigations, and watched to see if they would catch Jihadi John.

Jihadi John was finally revealed to be Mohammed Emwazi in February 2015. The media released a lot of details about him, including his immigration status, language background, and education level. This made it possible to compare the suggestions of voice experts with the reality, and see how accurate we had been, based simply on a rather rudimentary analysis of the way he spoke.

Emwazi was born to Iraqi parents 1988, and the family moved to the UK in 1994. They settled in West London, where he grew up, and which is the general area where MLE developed. This was consistent with the idea that he spoke with an MLE accent— a British accent.

I had been asked whether he was likely to be an immigrant. I had suggested that, if this was the case, he was more likely to be an earlier rather than a later immigrant. I made this suggestion based on the fact that his pronunciation was native-like for the accent he was heard speaking. This was shown to be true—arriving in the country in 1994 would make him around six years of age when he entered the country. He was an early immigrant.

Emwazi had graduated from the University of Westminster in London. My suggestion that he had been educated to university level, based on his general use of language, was also shown to be right.

I am the first one to agree that these attributes could belong to a large group of people. It's a bit like believing the characteristics in your Zodiac sign are an accurate picture of your personality, disposition, and characteristics; there's a lot of very general information in the profile for each of the twelve signs, and it can be interpreted to fit practically anyone. Even though Emwazi's mother had reportedly said she recognized the voice as her son's, we have to remember that experience with a voice is not enough to identify it as a particular person. Even evidence from voice line-ups, which are put together with meticulous care, has to be treated with caution. A more detailed forensic analysis would need to be carried out to ascertain how likely it was that Jihadi John and Mohammed Emwazi were one and the same person. In order for that to happen, the authorities would need to interview Emwazi so that there was a reference sample to which the speech from the videos could be compared. To this day, I am unsure whether that kind of comparison ever took place.

It's not just speaker comparison or profiling...

My colleague Peter French is a well-known forensic phonetician who runs his own firm carrying out forensic speech services. He is also responsible for first getting me involved in speech analysis when he was my phonetics lecturer at university.

I have heard Peter speak on a number of occasions about his work as a forensic phonetician. And it's not all about speaker comparison, speaker profiling, and voice line-ups. Some of the work has involved throwing a pig carcass down a stairwell in a block of flats, for example!

The reason for this is that Peter's firm is asked to work on a number of things involving what a witness claims to have heard. These can include, but are not limited to:

1. Working out what is said on a recording, rather than—or as well as—who said it.

2. Deciding whether it is possible for someone to have heard a certain phrase in a particular environment—e.g., could you really hear that much detail through the wall from a neighbouring property?

3. Testing whether a witness could have heard a body hit the ground from a certain height, and what this sounds like—hence using the carcass of a pig, similar in size and weight to a murder victim, rather than an actual human body.

4. Deciding whether a recording has been tampered with.

Let's have a look at some of these.

'Sorry—what was that?'

It can be pivotal in a case to work out exactly what was said, and whether a person could have heard a certain word or phrase. However, even experts disagree at times.

A good example of (non-expert) people hearing things differently is the Yanny/Laurel phenomenon.

In May 2018, the Internet was all a-flap about a recording which had been made for an online dictionary. Did the recording say *Yanny*, or did it say *Laurel*? If you search for 'Yanny Laurel' on the Internet, you can listen and try this out for yourself.[9]

It was utterly baffling to people who heard *Yanny* that others were hearing *Laurel*, and vice versa. A few people heard something in between but, for the most part, people heard one or the other with complete clarity. To my surprise, I heard *Yanny* when I listened to it on my desktop computer speakers, but *Laurel* on my mobile phone. In fact, there is a clue in that.

Apparently, the sound file was originally produced by a professional singer for an online dictionary along with a load of other sound files. The word he recorded was *Laurel*. To make it manageable and quick to download for online platforms, the file had to be compressed considerably. Compression degrades the acoustic cues in the file, as it takes out a lot of the information a person is listening for. Take out too much of the information, and the file becomes impossible to interpret. Take out a little less than enough, and interesting things start to happen.

It is possible to do compression of audio files in a way which is almost indiscernible to the human ear. You may know that CDs contain a compressed version of the original recording made in a studio. This is done by a computer which has been programmed with instructions about what a human ear can hear and selectively removes information that a listener will not miss. Have you ever heard people say vinyl records sound better than CDs? This is because the sound is not compressed when it is transferred to a vinyl record, and some people are sensitive to that. It may be one of the reasons vinyl records are so large in comparison with CDs.

The compression of the original Yanny/Laurel file was such that it seems to have selectively saved parts of the sound information in a way that caused listeners to hear different things. But your brain wants to make sense of speech, so it does its best to interpret what you are hearing.

Why did some people hear *Yanny*, and others hear *Laurel*? What follows is my suggestion. For a different take (that basically blows my suggestion out of the water), see forensic phonetician Helen Fraser's comprehensive blog post.[10]

If you cut out the lower frequencies of the recording, people tended to hear *Yanny*. Cutting out the higher frequencies caused people to hear *Laurel*. When people were listening to it and saying which they could hear, older people seemed more likely to hear *Yanny*. This could be because our hearing becomes worse over time as we age, with frequencies at the upper and lower end of the scale being eroded. As many of the frequencies for *Laurel* were near the lower end of a younger person's hearing spectrum, an older person might be less likely to hear *Laurel* and more likely to hear the higher frequencies in *Yanny*.

OK...so why did I hear *Yanny* on my computer speakers and *Laurel* on my phone?

This is probably because the lower end of the frequency spectrum is boosted on many mobile phones, as the speakers are very small. If you can hear someone's music through their headphones on the train, what you're normally hearing is all the high-frequency stuff—it sounds very 'tsss tsss tsss', rather than the 'boom boom boom' you get from some kind person in a convertible sharing the music on their car stereo with you. This is because the speakers in the headphones—particularly in-ear headphones—are tiny, and you have to have them right up close to your ear—or in it—to be able to hear the lower frequencies. So that you get a better experience of the sound when listening to the speakers on your mobile phone, the bass frequencies are artificially boosted. Boosting the bass signal is going to make *Laurel* jump to the fore. My mobile phone had suddenly taken years off my hearing age!

This has implications for hearing things accurately in all sorts of environments, and is one reason why forensic phoneticians are asked to give an expert opinion on what is said on some recordings, and whether a listener could have heard certain words spoken.

In noisy environments, you may well hear something differently from if it was spoken in quieter surroundings; it is possible to take some of the noise off recordings, but this needs to be done with care not to remove speech information. If someone is speaking very quickly, it can also be difficult to work out what was said, particularly if the speaker has unfamiliar accent features. Word boundaries can also be disputed. Did she say 'Bring the grey tape', or 'Bring the great ape'? This may be crucial to working out what happened in a crime.

If a witness claims to have overheard a certain word or phrase being shouted in a next-door flat, forensic phoneticians may be asked to work out whether that was possible. Barriers such as windows and walls allow some frequencies to pass—usually the lower frequencies—whereas others will not be able to. If a witness claims to have heard a speaker shouting 'Have you got a knife?', the speaker may have in fact been shouting something like 'Have you got it right?'. A forensic phonetician will not be able to say which phrase was shouted, but may well be able to work out whether it was possible for a listener to tell the difference between the two phrases.

As with all forensic work, two or more experts will be asked to examine the material and agree on their conclusions before an opinion can be offered with any degree of confidence. If agreement cannot be reached, then this can also be used in evidence.

A true record?

Forensic phoneticians can also be asked how reliable a particular recording is—i.e., whether evidence has been tampered with. In fraud cases, for example, someone may present a recording of a conversation which they state is reliable, but the other person in the recording disputes having said a certain thing or agreed to something. This makes it important to work out whether the recording is an accurate representation of the facts.

An example might be an edit to the very simplistic exchange below:

A1: So we're going to move the £200 from your savings account to your current account.

B1: Yes.

A2: And do you want to close the savings account and transfer the balance to my savings account?

B2: No.

A3: So we're agreed then.

B3: Yes, I'm happy with that.

If speaker A has the only copy of the recording and alters the 'no' response at B2 to 'yes' by copying it from B1, speaker B is now (erroneously) agreeing to close their savings account and transfer the balance to A's saving's account.

A1: So we're going to move the £200 from your savings account to your current account.

B1: Yes. ← copied]

A2: And do you want to close the savings account and transfer the balance to my savings account?

B2: Yes. ← pasted from B1 above]

A3: So we're agreed then.

B3: Yes, I'm happy with that.

How would a forensic phonetician go about ascertaining that this recording had been tampered with?

Earlier in this chapter, I demonstrated that the same word spoken by the same person more than once has different spectral features, using the example of me saying *bumblebee* three times in a row. A forensic phonetician would look at the spectral images of the word *yes* in B2 and see how similar it was to the one in B1. If it was identical, that is so unlikely that it would call into question the reliability of the recording.

In a case I looked at with colleagues, words and phrases had been spliced into a recording from one made at another time in a different place between the same two speakers. The recording had been used to blackmail one of the speakers and had been done very cleverly from the point of view of constructing a convincing conversation. While it was not immediately apparent to the human ear, examining the spectral information of the file clearly showed background noise in the spliced sections that was not present in the rest of the recording and was not perceptible to the human ear. Had this not been subject to forensic analysis, the anomalies in the recording would quite possibly never have come to light.

It is possible to be more certain in these kinds of cases as the forensic evidence is much less open to dispute—much less variable, less open to interpretation, and more like a fingerprint in that respect. Forensic speech analysis on the whole always carries caveats, however. It may look like a very straightforward task to judge a person based on the way they speak, but—as I have tried to show—voice and speech analysis is in fact a very complex area.

In Chapter 6, we're going to look at people whose voices are re-made to one extent or another. These are people who feel they need to be judged differently for a variety of reasons, and have made choices about their voices based on that. This highlights the complexity of voice and identity in a way we have not yet considered... and it's utterly fascinating.

CHAPTER 6

Making a change
Transgender speech and synthesized voices

S ophie[1] sets her guitar down after coming off stage at the pub. It's a Thursday night, and she's hosting a showcase for local musicians. Her band has just played a cracking thirty-minute set of original and cover songs to open the evening, which was met with thunderous applause. The pub is heaving with people who have come to see her band, come to see other bands, or just fancied a good night out.

The band members from the next act emerge from the crowd and start unzipping their instrument cases. There's an amount of confusion while the musicians look for electric sockets to plug their effects pedals into; guitars are tuned and drums positioned. Sophie puts her guitar away and waits patiently by the stage, offering help: there's a four-way over here; move the monitor so it's facing you properly; do you need another microphone stand? And so on.

While she's waiting for the next act to get set up and be ready so she can introduce them, a woman appears from the other side of the bar, looking around for someone. She approaches Sophie, seeming a bit puzzled and still clearly looking for someone else.

'Do you know the band—the one that was just on?' she says. 'I wanted to tell the singer how brilliant he was.'

Sophie blinks and draws breath. This could go a number of ways. 'I am the singer,' she says.

'Oh!' The woman does a double take. She looks abashed. 'I was stuck behind the bar over there and I couldn't see you.'

Then, after a moment, she says brightly: 'Well, you were fab. Does your band play parties?'

This chapter looks at people who have had some kind of voice change or disconnect. It starts by looking at (mainly) male-to-female transgender speakers, before moving on to consider the issues around the use of synthetic voices among people who are unable to produce speech themselves for some reason—think Stephen Hawking, and you'll understand what I mean.

What these people have in common is that they have all had to think quite consciously about whether their voices represent them because of some kind of change in their voice or in their identity, or because they have to choose how they want to sound. For some, it doesn't matter very much. For others, it is a vital part of who they are.

Transgender voices

I didn't hate being a boy; I just knew I wasn't one.

Paula Stone Williams. Pastor of Preaching
and Worship, Left Hand Church[2]

Simply stated, transgender individuals are those who know they are not themselves in the biologically gendered body they were born with. They could realize this as children, young people, or later on in life. In a TEDx video by Susie Green, CEO of the charity Mermaids and also simply a mum talking about her daughter Jackie's transgender journey, Susie tells us that Jackie told her when she was four years old that God had 'made a mistake'.[3]

While this realization may not lead to dramatic outward physical change in some, it can lead someone to decide to live their life as a person of the other gender, and can involve taking hormones to change their physical appearance, often in the run-up to undergoing surgery to effect physical change.

People who do not experience these feelings and are content to live life in the gender they were born with are known as cisgender individuals.

Being transgender is by no means a simple issue, though—and not something I can go into in great detail in this book. What we are interested in here is whether transgender people feel their voice represents the gender identity they have assumed. The 'not simple' part is that transgender individuals do not necessarily want to sound like a cisgender person. For example, a male to female transgender person may not want to sound like a cisgender woman, although many do.

There has been research on transgender voices going back to the 1970s at least. A fascinating dissertation by Sidney Wong[4] on transmasculine voice (i.e. the voice in female-to-male transgender speakers), written as part of his Master of Arts degree in 2017, summarizes the studies into transgender voice, starting with an observation by researcher Ralph Coleman in 1983 that 'the gender characteristic most resistant to convincing change is the voice'. In 1995, Deborah Günzburger observed that convincing change of the voice is still difficult, particularly so for male-to-female transsexuals.[5]

Coleman had been working on transgender voice since the 1970s. He points out that, while the obvious difference between male and female voice might be pitch—in that women's voices tend to have a higher average pitch than men's voices, and that is something people listen for when making a judgement about gender—there is more to it than just asking a transfeminine (male-to-female) speaker to speak with a higher pitch or a transmasculine speaker to assume a lower pitch. Deborah Günzburger is in complete agreement. She explains that male children develop adult male speech habits and female children develop adult female speech habits a long time before puberty, and that this involves differences in the articulation of speech sounds as well as voice pitch.

Having said that, studies such as the ones carried out by James Hillenbrand and Michael Clarke in the late 2000s showed that pitch was more important than other factors when asking listeners to identify speaker gender.[6] They used synthesized voices to test this, and started with voices which were typical of cisgender males. They then altered two features of the voices, the pitch and the vowel space, to be close to typical values for cisgender female speakers. Listeners were presented with the following types of voices:

a. the synthesized male (original) voices;
b. the original voices with the pitch only moved up towards the female range;
c. the original voices with the vowel space only modified to be like the female vowel space;
d. the original voices with both the pitch and the vowel space modifications.

Listeners then had to decide whether they thought the speech was more male-sounding or more female-sounding.

You might be thinking, 'What's this about vowel space?' in option (c).

Basically, cisgender women tend to have smaller mouths than cisgender men, and this means the way they produce vowels is slightly different. This has an effect on the acoustic output and the way listeners perceive vowels. In a synthesized voice, it's possible to manipulate the acoustic features of vowels to make them sound more like how a woman would speak them and, therefore, how someone would perceive the vowels.

It's a similar situation with pitch. Cisgender men's voices are generally lower than cisgender women's because, as we saw in Chapters 1 and 3, men tend to have a larger larynx, or voice box, than women. The larynx develops during puberty, when the voice 'breaks' in men and suddenly becomes much lower in pitch. It also develops in women, but not to the same extent, and not usually with an obvious 'break'. We know that cisgender men have an average pitch of around 100–150 Hz, and that cisgender women's voices tend to be around 200–300 Hz.

As I've already mentioned, transgender people usually have some kind of hormone therapy. Transmasculine people are administered the male hormone testosterone. Among other physical changes associated with increased testosterone levels, the larynx will usually start to change, as in male puberty. Transmasculine men experience some of the changes associated with cisgender male puberty, and this is usually one of them. It means that transmasculine speakers often end up with a lower average pitch than before taking the hormones simply because of physical changes to the larynx.

Female hormones progesterone and oestrogen, taken by trans-feminine people, cannot reverse changes in the larynx which have already taken place to an individual during puberty. If you know before you hit puberty that you're transgender—and many young people do—it is possible to have treatment which pauses puberty; Sophie refers to 'puberty blockers'. Once you stop taking puberty blockers, normal puberty processes resume. Puberty blockers may well mitigate any changes to the voice in transfeminine pre-adolescents. At the moment, though, it seems that the majority of people do not take puberty blockers for a variety of reasons, and so transfeminine speakers are forced to deal with having an adult male larynx.

In Jackie Green's case, mum Susie describes the horror and anguish Jackie went through as a teenager when she realized her voice was starting to break. From Susie's account, it does not seem puberty blockers were readily available from the UK National Health Service at the time (we're probably looking at the mid-2000s), and so the family was forced to seek treatment in the United States. Fortunately for Jackie, it seems that any large-scale change in the larynx stopped once she started taking the puberty blockers.

Physical differences are not the whole story, however. There are cultural and societal factors which shape the male and female voice, and which could also be responsible in part for the way cisgender speakers say their vowels and use their pitch. For example, in Japan, women are traditionally encouraged to use high-pitch voices—sometimes unnaturally high—as it sounds more feminine or 'gentle'. Deborah Günzburger explains that women in Sweden produce the Swedish word for *yes*—'ja'—on an in-breath, whereas Swedish men do not. We saw in Chapter 3 how English-speaking cisgender men and women use their voices very differently in an attempt to attract sexual partners or show certain kinds of social allegiances, and this can vary quite a lot between cultures.

Hillenbrand and Clarke found that the best results for getting people to assign a female gender to the speakers was to manipulate both pitch and vowel space. Pitch on its own and vowel space on its own were not effective... BUT pitch was the more important cue out of the two of them.

A very small-scale piece of research I did with my colleague Rodney Jones and student research assistant Iona Jacob used real speech, as opposed to synthesized speech, to test which features of the voice correlated with a series of speaker characteristics. We looked at a number of characteristics, including male, female, strong, educated, intelligent, caring, and so on. We were really only interested in whether listeners identified speakers as male or female, and added in the other characteristics mainly as foils.

Rodney and I asked Iona to make recordings of five speakers reading a short story, Aesop's fable *The North Wind and the Sun*. The speakers were one each of the following: transmasculine, transfeminine, cismasuline, cisfeminine, and a person who identified as having a fluid gender identity and who was biologically female.

We then sent the link to the survey out on social media (were you one of the respondents?). More than 170 people from all over the world rated the speakers.

You may be wondering why we chose that story.

The North Wind and the Sun is a passage traditionally used in phonetic research. For example, the phonetic and phonological descriptions of languages appearing in the *Handbook of the International Phonetic Association*[7] are based on speakers of those languages reciting the story in their own languages. We wanted to keep the content the same for each speaker, and the passage had to be as neutral and straightforward as possible, and so we picked *The North Wind and the Sun*. We acknowledge there were likely to be some differences in narrative style.

When we looked at the how the listeners had rated the speakers, the feature which correlated most closely with whether a speaker was perceived to be male or female was average pitch. If you remember, we expect the average pitch to be around 100 Hz for cisgender men, and 200–300 Hz for cisgender women— so, more or less double. The transfeminine speaker, who had the lowest average pitch at around 90 Hz, was judged by the participants as being most likely to be male, based on the listening task alone. The transmasculine and cismasculine speakers were also judged to be male by most listeners; they also had relatively low average pitch, slightly higher than the transfeminine speaker in the 100–110 Hz range. The cisfeminine and fluid gender speakers were both judged likely to be female. They had a much higher average pitch than any of the other speakers, both within the 200–250 Hz range associated with cisgender women.

The fact that the listeners judged the transfeminine speaker as most likely to be male reminded me of something that had happened at an event I attended on the voice in London in 2016. *This is a voice* at the Wellcome Collection[8] showcased work by artists and vocalists about the voice in communication and in society, with an emphasis on non-verbal communication. There were various different sorts of exhibits, including video installations, sculpture, photography, painting, with medical illustrations and manuscripts mixed in.

There was also a series of vocal exercises to try to help look after and enhance your voice. You can find these in the accompanying book by Gillyanne Kayes and Jeremy Fisher.[9]

This is totally my kind of thing. I went to the website to get tickets, filled with excitement.

The tickets had all gone.

I then found out that my colleague Jonnie Robinson was involved in a panel discussion on the voice and representation as part of the *This is a voice* exhibition. Jonnie is the lead curator of the spoken English collection at the British Library and is enormously knowledgeable about accents of English. I persuaded Jonnie to get me on to the guest list for the panel discussion. Thank you, Jonnie.

Of the speakers, one was a transfeminine actor, Rebecca Root, who spoke about her voice. Even though she has done work on national television, I hadn't seen her before and didn't know she was transgender. When she started speaking, I thought her voice was quite low in pitch...but there could have been a number of reasons why she was part of the panel, her relatively low-pitched voice being one. I also thought she might be doing it on purpose as an actor to make a point—something like, 'when I speak like this I sound more masculine'. When it became apparent that she was transfeminine and was there to speak about that aspect of the voice, the low pitch made sense to me from a voice perspective. Aside from that, I didn't think her language was particularly stereotypically male or female.

At the end of the evening, a blind person in the audience approached Rebecca and appears to have told her that all he could hear when she spoke was the voice of a man.

When we're talking to people, visual cues are really important. If you can see a person that you perceive to be a woman (or a man) in front of you when that person is speaking, you are likely to take the whole package on board and reconcile any anomalies. There have even been studies which showed that voices were perceived more or less favourably when people were presented with pictures of different people but heard the same voice and asked to rate the speaker. As our study and the one by Hillenbrand and Clarke show, if you can't see a speaker but can only hear them, the voice is a compelling cue that listeners will rely on in order to work out the identity of the person they are speaking to. An obvious instance in which you might be likely to hear someone and not see them is on the phone—and we saw the kind of assumption people can make in general in Chapter 3, when my friend Heather had built up a mental image of my then boyfriend which was utterly wrong, just from hearing his voice on the phone. And we also saw an example of not being able to see someone in the opening scenario to this chapter, when Sophie was thought to be a man by someone who couldn't see her singing.

If people are incorrectly perceived as belonging to one or other gender—either through their voice, the way they look, or a combination of things—this is known as 'misgendering'.

It was really interesting to hear Rebecca speaking about the strategies she adopted so that she was not misgendered by her voice—particularly on the phone, when the listener does not have the strong visual cue that a person has a particular gender identity. She explained that she makes her voice sound more breathy. My friend Sophie told me that she always starts phone calls with 'Hi, this is Sophie', particularly if she doesn't know the person she is calling (or who has called her), as this is a feminine name and the listener is less likely to misgender her.

For many transgender people—and certainly all the ones I have spoken to—being misgendered because of their voice is very upsetting. They could interpret this in a number of ways. For example, they can interpret it as an indication that they are not successful in assuming their intended gender identity. Sidney Wong's research reveals that transmasculine speakers who were not misgendered over the phone felt more masculine, perceived their own voice as 'very male', and expressed greater satisfaction that their voice represented them as male, not female. Transmasculine speakers who were misgendered as female were less likely to feel that way. Wong also reported that decreasing instances of misgendering over the phone contributed to transmasculine speakers' growing confidence and their likeliness of ultimately living in their intended male gender identity. This reminds me of something Paula Stone Williams says in her TEDx talk about women starting to doubt themselves when men question their knowledge or beliefs. If you've grown up a transgender man in a female body, and may have had to be outwardly female while growing up, you'll be used to having your knowledge and beliefs questioned, because that's just what happens to women. Having consistent proof that your voice sounds like a male voice will help you be confident in that persona.

Another possible interpretation of being misgendered because of your voice is that the listener has done it deliberately, and that it is a straightforward form of prejudice against transgender people. I know Sophie has encountered this and has been very upset by it. The scenario I gave at the start was not deliberate misgendering and, while Sophie feels disappointed that her singing voice does not sound feminine enough to avoid this kind of thing, and upset to have been misgendered, she does not blame people for this kind of mistake. Deliberate misgendering can happen for all sorts of reasons, but I am not going to go into that in this book. Let's stick to the voice.

We interviewed all the speakers from our study, at the same time as getting them to record *The North Wind and the Sun*, to find out how they felt about their voices and what sort of experiences they had had. What did they think of their voice? Had they gone through speech therapy, or had any kind of vocal support classes? Had people commented on their voice, favourably or unfavourably? Had they been misgendered as a result of their voice? While we didn't include their voices in the research, I also recorded and interviewed Sophie, who is transfeminine, and another transfeminine friend of a friend from the United States.

I'm going to start by saying this: Why don't people like the sound of their voices? Almost everyone I have interviewed for this book has said they don't like their voice. It doesn't matter if they are a radio personality, a singer, a trans- or cisgender person...Nobody seems to like their own voice! I suppose it's not that unreasonable; people don't like other physical things about themselves. Their nose, for example. Or having too much of a belly. Or not being tall enough. But: seriously people. Your voice is you. Learn to love it!

An article in *The Guardian* newspaper on this very topic[10]—people not liking the sound of their own voice—says this is partly because we hear our voice differently when we are speaking, so we don't really know what it sounds like to others. We don't only hear our voice through our ears, as a listener would do; we perceive it through resonances conducted through the bones in the face, head, and body. The result of this is that we think our voice is much deeper than it actually is.

Think about it; if you are playing music on your phone, it sounds different when you hold it in your hand and when you listen with in-ear headphones. I mentioned this in Chapter 5. In your hand, it sounds quite 'tinny'—you're hearing the high frequencies more. This is mainly because the built-in speaker in your phone is rather small, and is better at conveying higher frequencies than lower ones. In-ear headphones use the fact that they are in your ears to give you a better bass response. They interact with the bones in your skull to resonate at lower frequency levels so you can hear the bass better.

In the article, psychologist Silke Paulmann suggests that, when we hear a recording of our voice—i.e., as it sounds to others—we do not hear the same, more bassy sound that we're used to. The voice simply does not meet our expectations, and this means we don't like it. 'Our voice plays a massive role in forming our identity and I guess no one likes to realize that you're not really who you think you are,' she says.

The transgender speakers we interviewed are no different from anyone else in this respect. None of them said they liked their voice. I guess, in the case of transgender speakers, there is the added dimension that they may feel their voices don't represent the gender they identify with. This didn't seem to be the main issue, though. They just didn't like their voices.

I've been reflecting on whether or not I like my own voice as I write this. I don't dislike it, but I think I'm probably just used to it. The thing which annoys me most when I hear myself speaking on the radio is not the voice itself, but the number of hesitation fillers I use, like 'um' and 'er'. I've tried not to do this on radio interviews, but it's actually quite hard to avoid doing it as it is part of natural, spontaneous speech. We use hesitation fillers to stop someone from taking over the conversational turn when we're trying to think of what to say, for example. Something else I didn't realize I did so much was use 'So,...' to start sentences when I'm lecturing; that was only revealed to me when I made lecture videos for my students. Even BBC Breakfast had a segment on how annoying it is when people start sentences with 'So,...'. (Must try harder.)

Maybe the reason I don't dislike my voice—rather than disliking other aspects of the way that I speak—is because I've been listening to recordings of it since I was a child. My father gave me a tape recorder as a present when I was about ten years old. I know more or less what to expect and am fairly secure about how I sound and whether it represents me. I'm also regularly asked to provide speech recordings for pronunciation materials, speech experiments, and even for a friend's progressive rock album (*Redacted* by Also Eden). This makes me think that my voice must be quite nice, or people wouldn't want it.

Let's get back to my transgender interviewees.

Apart from Sophie, who has said I can give her name, I'm going to give each of my transgender interviewees an alias.

We'll call the British transfeminine speaker 'Karen'. The American transfeminine speaker will be referred to as 'Christine'. And the British transmasculine speaker will be known as 'Scott'.

I've chosen 'Christine' for the American transfeminine speaker as her real name, when abbreviated, could be either male or female, and she usually goes by the shortened version—the equivalent of 'Chris'. She told me she uses the full name at work to deliberately reinforce the fact that she is female and to avoid opportunities for misgendering.

What I was digging around trying to find out with the interviews is whether the speakers thought their voices represented them in the gender they identified with, and what sort of voice-related issues they had become aware of. These could be social issues—i.e., involving other people—or things they had experienced as their voices changed, or they changed their voices, to represent themselves during and following transition. As your voice is often something you don't really think about that much unless you've had cause to, I was interested in whether the importance of the voice as part of the representation of who a person is had come to the fore for transgender people. The transfeminine actor, Rebecca Root, at the Wellcome Collection event had clearly thought about her voice, but—as we have seen in Chapter 4 on professional voice users—we'd expect actors to have had vocal training, and so she was likely to be mindful about her voice anyway.

The discussion—although probably not all that surprising given previous research—threw up some interesting things.

Female-to-male: Scott

Let's start by looking at Scott's experience. It seems to have been pretty similar to that of the transmasculine speakers in Sydney Wong's research. The lower in pitch his voice gets, and the more he is recognized as male and not female, the better he feels. But he has not experienced a lot of difficulty, or much misgendering, since he assumed his masculine identity.

Scott identified as male when he was sixteen, and decided pretty much straight away to start hormone therapy treatment, which he did when he was nineteen. That was over a year before the interview. At the time of recording, he had not had any operations, but was living as a man. Iona has kept in touch with him and tells me he has since had his first operation.

Scott reflected on the effect of the hormone therapy treatment on his voice after Iona played him his recording of *The North Wind and the Sun.*

'It's much deeper than I thought. But when I talk to my friends, I get excited and it will crack or it might go a bit high-pitched. It's horrible and everyone laughs at me! But my voice is still changing.' He explains how he has asked people whether his voice is getting deeper. 'I like to know if it's got deeper. One friend said it's got deeper from New Year's, which is surprising, 'cos that's six months.'

Scott definitely prefers his voice to sound deeper, and the fact that it sounds deeper than he thought in the recording, coupled with the prospect of it getting even lower in pitch, is something which pleases him. 'I might drop it some more and that makes me happy.'

The fact that other people—particularly men—have identified him as being male is also something he attributes in part to his voice. He talks about a time he visited Iona's student digs. 'I went to your house and [your cismasculine flatmate] was just like "Who's that guy you've got over?" That was surprising because I didn't think that my voice had dropped that much.' Scott says he actually avoided talking to people in public during the first year of hormone therapy because he wasn't confident about his voice and whether it would affect how he wanted people to perceive him. 'Now my voice has dropped, I feel like I'm definitely more confident in public.' On being misgendered: 'Some people think like 'cos I'm shorter they'll be, "Oh maybe that's a girl with short hair", but normally, when I talk, they change it back.' His voice is definitely preventing people from misgendering him.

What sort of conscious strategies does Scott adopt, if any, to make his voice sound more male? Pitch range is the key, he thinks—not so much pitch average. 'You kind of make it monotone.' This means he keeps the melody quite flat. Wider pitch range, indicating increased expression or emotional involvement, is a feminine attribute of the voice, and therefore to be avoided.

During the conversation, Scott says that he hates hearing the sound of his voice before starting hormone therapy. Iona reveals that he made a video called *Six Months on T*—six months on testosterone. It's worth searching for 'six months on testosterone' on YouTube, as there are lots of fascinating videos made by people transitioning from female to male under this title. The one produced by Ryan Flores,[11] for example, has a section on how his voice sounds in the first, second, third, fourth, fifth, and sixth months on testosterone. In the first month, his average pitch is at 135 Hz, which is already in the average male range, if slightly towards the upper end. By the sixth month, his pitch average is 94 Hz. That's a considerable drop, and will almost unequivocally be perceived by listeners as being male.

Throughout the interview, Scott seems pretty satisfied with his voice. He makes the observation that transgender women 'have it harder' because hormone therapy cannot change the voice once male puberty has taken place. And it's in Scott's interview that the issue of transgender women not necessarily wanting to sound cisfeminine comes up.

Scott identifies as bisexual. When he was doing his research before deciding to start hormone therapy, one of the things he was interested in was sexuality as well as gender. He came across the case of a transfeminine person who identified as lesbian. 'She'd gone through speech therapy. And she was annoyed that they would only teach her how to speak like a straight cisgender woman, and not like a lesbian. That wasn't what she wanted.' This person had clearly noticed that there are differences in how lesbian and straight cisgender women speak, and wanted to reflect that as part of her identity. As I mentioned earlier in this chapter: it's complicated.

Male-to-female: Sophie, Christine, and Karen

I've got three times as much data from transfeminine speakers than from transmasculine ones—literally, three transfeminine speakers and one transmasculine speaker. When Rodney, Iona, and I set out to do the research, it became evident that this was in proportion with male-to-female and female-to-male transition rates in Europe—that is, three times as many individuals undergo male-to-female gender reassignment as undergo female-to-male gender reassignment.

The reasons for this are harder to explain. One account suggests that it is because women can perform almost the entirety of a male gender role without having to undergo gender reassignment surgery. It is simply more acceptable in society for women to dress in a masculine way—or, indeed, as a man—than it is for men to dress as women. There are many accounts in historical record of women successfully disguising themselves as men and living a male life; a quick look on the Internet gives an example as far back as the sixth century, when a father successfully disguised his daughter as a son, taking the child to a monastery so that they could both become monks. Born in the late 1700s, James Barry, born Margaret Anne Bulkley, became a military surgeon in the British army in the 1800s. This was at a time when women were not permitted to train and qualify as medical doctors. The fact that James was a woman was not discovered until death.

The transfeminine speakers we interviewed were at different points in their transition. Karen had not started taking hormones, and was in the position where they were a man at home (we'll call their male persona 'Kevin') and only Karen at work. At the time we interviewed Karen, they were describing themselves as a 'transgender person' rather than a transgender woman, and so I have used the personal pronoun 'they' to refer to Karen. Both Christine and Sophie had transitioned and been through surgery, Christine several years before and Sophie relatively recently—although both were keen to stress this is a lengthy process and the journey does not stop once you have had surgery. Both Christine and Sophie identified with the pronoun 'she'. None of them—Karen, Christine, nor Sophie—had had laryngeal surgery to change the size and shape of their voice boxes and, while Christine and Sophie had tried some speech therapy, they had both abandoned it fairly quickly. None of them had had extensive vocal coaching.

The only one of this trio of female-to-male transgender people who likes their voice is Christine, and there might be a reason for that. Like me, Christine has studied linguistics extensively, and so is familiar with the sound of her own voice. She also says she is able to accept her own voice, which I take to mean she feels that her voice represents who she is. She also finds it reassuring that people she interacts with have said they like her voice. I can identify with that!

Christine is also able to be quite analytical about her voice, because she has the terminology to do so. When we discuss whether she thinks she has consciously changed her voice from how she spoke before she decided to transition, she says she thinks she has, on three main counts. Firstly, she thinks she raises her pitch. She comments that she finds this quite tiring, however—and even suggests I compare her pitch at the start and end of the interview to see if it has dropped back down again. I measure it. It hasn't. It's actually increased slightly, from around 102 Hz on average at the start to around 115 Hz on average near the end. This is not a huge difference, and certainly not a difference of the 100 Hz kind. However, I don't have any recordings of her before transition.

Secondly, Christine says she believes she is more breathy than she was before transitioning. The third thing is that she says she deliberately tries to use creaky voice because she knows it is something associated with young women, even though it is so strongly criticized by the press as being ugly.

This all indicates that Christine believes the voice is an important part of her transition, and changing it to some extent is necessary in order to be able to fully assume her female identity. But that's not the same for everyone.

In contrast with Christine, Karen doesn't think they change their voice much. At the time of interview, they are more focused on how they look physically than how they sound, so they haven't paid the voice much attention. They say they have always been reasonably softly spoken, even in their male persona— although some colleagues have commented that Karen becomes even more softly spoken (even difficult to hear!) as Karen.

An issue for Karen is that they doubt they can actually change their voice, as they don't feel they have much control over it. This stems from a school pantomime performance in Year 6, when Karen's teacher announced that Karen's (then Kevin's) was the worst singing voice she had heard. Since then, Karen has never liked their voice, but isn't clear what they can do to change it. Iona conducted this interview; she offers that a transgender friend was told by a speech therapist that we change our voices all the time depending on whom we're speaking with, and whether we notice it or not. This might give Karen a bit of hope that she can control her voice. Karen is pretty firm that the voice is not the priority at the moment, though—outward appearances matter more. They have a startlingly impressive collection of nail varnish in their office. 'It's a bit of a thing,' says Karen.

In our interview, Sophie is quite clear how she feels. 'The voice gives everything away,' she says. 'People assume so much from what they hear. They get a lot of information from the way someone speaks. It's got a much bigger role than it should have!' Being a singer, Sophie is also quite aware of how her voice sounds; it's a bit softer, higher in pitch, and has more pitch range than her previous male voice, and she has worked consciously to change it. We talk about the difference between singing and speaking, and how she wishes she could sound more feminine with her singing voice, to avoid the kind of scenario I presented at the start of this chapter. But she also wants to get more volume out and not tire her voice so much during a performance. When I propose lowering the larynx to reduce sub-glottal pressure, and trying high and low notes with it down there rather than up here, she objects. 'I was told to tilt the larynx higher to sound more feminine!' she says. Raising the larynx makes the vocal cavity smaller and, therefore, more similar to a woman's in size. That will have an effect on how speech sounds and whether a speaker is perceived as being male or female. It's a shame we didn't have Sophie's recording for our small-scale study, as I'm sure the results would have been interesting. Singing with a raised larynx is not going to increase the cavity to provide greater resonance and volume, though. Having said that, she gets a lot of compliments about her singing voice, she says.

Another topic we discussed with the transfeminine group was the role of the voice in misgendering. Both Sophie and Karen use the strategy of mentioning their names at the start of telephone conversations with people they don't know to help remove any ambiguity for the other speaker. Until recently, Karen was sometimes at work as Kevin and sometimes as Karen, and Karen says colleagues have difficulty knowing which name to use on the phone largely for this reason, rather than because of the voice. 'A lot of my confidence (being Karen) comes from other people's confidence with me,' says Karen. It has become increasingly easier to be Karen successfully with their colleagues at work, although there are still some people who always use the male name when she is dressed as Karen. That annoys her—and is, quite frankly and as Iona points out, extremely disrespectful—and it can also sap her confidence. But it's not a voice issue.

Sophie has experienced intentional and unintentional misgendering based on her voice. There's a dramatized example of what happened with her singing voice at the start of this chapter; she is annoyed by this and a bit disappointed when it happens, as it makes it seem clear that her voice is not representing her as a woman. But she does not feel the person doing it is being intentionally rude. Taxi drivers are another matter. 'I've been deliberately misgendered by taxi drivers, despite being very visually female,' she says. She is also misgendered in taxis when she gets into the back of a black cab and the driver is not paying attention. 'It's just rude,' she says.

Christine's experiences of being misgendered are also not usually intentional on the other person's part. She works in computer programming and says the uniform is basically jeans and a t-shirt, which can look quite androgynous. She's been 'Sir-ed' several times when dressed like that, she says, particularly when she's had her hair up in a cap, but has also been 'Ma'am-ed' when wearing the same clothes. The most bizarre time she has been misgendered was when she was dressed in a blouse and a skirt and someone referred to her as 'Sir'. She says she can't think of any reason why they would do that other than the effect of her voice. But she's not sure that was the reason. To help people at work to address her as 'Ma'am' and not 'Sir', she introduces herself as Christine and not Chris, even though she uses the abbreviated version with all her friends. She also says she thinks how someone looks is generally more of a dominant cue than how someone sounds.

Both Christine and Karen have interesting comments to make about visual versus audio cues to someone's identity. Karen mentions how people reacted differently to the Kennedy/Nixon debate broadcasts in the 1960s, when both were standing for US President. People who watched the debates on television generally preferred Kennedy, who was good-looking and knew how to present himself for a visual audience, whereas those who heard them on the radio generally preferred Nixon, whose voice had more gravitas. Christine once did a test which looked at people's ability to tell the difference between voices and faces, and she did much better with faces, which tended to be the trend. As humans are predisposed to recognize faces from a very early age, this could explain why visual images of people are more compelling than voices in most situations. And as far as presentation skills are concerned, how you look is more important than the sound of your voice or what you say, according to research done by Albert Mehrabian in the 1960s, published in 1971.[12]

Figure 16 is a pictorial representation of what Mehrabian found. In it, you can see that how you look is the most important thing, followed by how you sound, and only then by what you say.

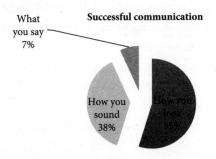

Figure 16 Visual adaptation of Mehrabian's model of successful communication

This would rather confirm that—as Karen suggests—visual cues 'trump' audio ones. However, as Karen also says, 'if the voice is difficult to take seriously, it will undermine the message.' That's probably why Mrs Thatcher had vocal coaching; her tendency to become rather high-pitched when she was passionate about something caused (male) politicians to ridicule her, and that undermined her cause and her ambitions.

So, what have we learned from this small sample of four people?

First and foremost, the voice does play a part in how transgender individuals are perceived, and in how they view themselves. Most of the interviewees expressed high levels of satisfaction when people correctly identified them as belonging to their chosen gender based on their voices. But, although speech therapy and coaching is available to transgender individuals, none of the people I interviewed had taken it up in any seriousness. Both Christine and Sophie had given it a go, but neither of them found it satisfactory. Anecdotal evidence from Scott, about the lesbian transfeminine speaker feeling disappointed when a speech therapist tried to make her sound like a cisgender woman, points to the fact that gender identities are extremely complex; it cannot be assumed that the main aim of a transgender person is to 'pass' successfully as someone from the cisgender population. It also underlines the subconscious bias of cisgender individuals. Basically, people shouldn't make assumptions about a person's gender just by hearing the sound of their voice.

Constructed voices

I remember the first time I heard the voice of Professor Stephen Hawking. It was in an episode of *Star Trek: The Next Generation* entitled 'Descent', first broadcast in 1993. At the start of this episode, before the credits run, he appears playing poker with the android character, Data, and eminent physicists Albert Einstein and Isaac Newton. And he's telling a joke.

I then heard him on the 1994 Pink Floyd album *The Division Bell*, where some of his speech is used on the song 'Keep Talking'. Here are the first few lines:

For millions of years, mankind lived just like the animals. Then something happened which unleashed the power of our imagination: we learned to talk.

This brilliant man, with a severe pathology (motor neurone disease), who could no longer produce speech using his vocal apparatus, actively demonstrated the power and importance of speech, language, and communication ... and he did that through a speech synthesizer.

Even once his condition had started to deteriorate in earnest, Hawking was still able to speak to some extent, and relied on people who knew him and could understand him to translate for him. However, in 1985, he lost the ability to speak after a period of pneumonia—and near death—required him to have a tracheotomy so he could breathe. A tracheotomy involves cutting open the throat and inserting a tube into the trachea (windpipe), usually just below the larynx. But for someone whose speech abilities are already impeded owing to his motor neurone disease, this must have been enough to put paid to natural speech for good.

To help him communicate effectively, Hawking was given a speech synthesis program in 1986, which initially worked on a desktop computer. It involved him selecting words, letters, and phrases by hand from a bank of around 3,000, which the program would read out in a process known as 'text to speech', or

TTS. This was developed and adapted over the years, first to be operated from a keyboard attached to his wheelchair, and eventually, as his condition worsened, to respond to movements of muscles in his face. It also used predictive technology of the kind we now have in our smartphone keyboards—including the fun and games associated with autocorrect, one assumes! The developers of the computer systems scanned in large numbers of Hawking's research papers so the software could make accurate predictions of what he might want to say (or write) based on his observed language patterns. This helped ease the process of producing speech and language.

The voice Hawking used from the speech synthesis program he was given in 1986 had an American accent, and has long been discontinued. I'm assuming that any number of people who were using this software also used this voice, meaning, at the time, the voice was not unique to Hawking. In later years, a greater number of voices of different types and with different accents have become available. The idea of this choice was to allow people to select something they felt represented them better.

But Hawking decided to stick with the voice he had been given at the start. It had become his voice. When he was asked why his voice had an American accent—given he was a British scientist— he said, 'I keep it because I have not heard a voice I like better and because I have identified with it.'

And now...well, it's an iconic voice. If there were anybody still using this voice, none of them is likely to have had the kind of media coverage that Hawking has had. If you hear it, you know it is the voice of Stephen Hawking. It is part of his lasting identity.

In the next section, I'm going to look at some of the basic issues to do with speech synthesis, and how a synthesized voice can be used to represent a person who is unable to speak for one reason or another.

Think about it: literally having no voice. How would that make you feel? It's bad enough when you get a cold and lose your voice, but you know it will eventually come back. This section considers those who have either lost their voice for good, or never really had one in the first place.

Speech synthesis: a very brief introduction

Scientists have been building speech synthesizers since the late 1700s, when Hungarian inventor Wolfgang von Kempelen built something he called his 'Speaking Machine'. It used bellows to represent the lungs, rubber tubing for the oral and nasal cavities, and a reed from a woodwind instrument, such as a clarinet, to replicate the vocal folds. Squeezing the bellows would push air through the reed, which would then make a note. Manipulating the rubber tubing at various points meant von Kempelen could get the model to produce words and phrases which listeners seemed able to perceive correctly. Because his Speaking Machine had only one reed, however, von Kempelen was unable to change the pitch of the speech, and so it always sounded monotone. Contemporary reports suggest that he decided the next lot of experimenters could work on that particular challenge.

If you want to get an idea of how different tube shapes can result in different vowel sounds, Exploratorium's web page 'Vocal Vowels' has some interactive material you can try. They use a duck call as the vocal folds. Scan the QR code image below, and then click on the pictures of the duck call and the shaped tubes, and you can hear different vowel sounds. It's really quite uncanny! The page also had a comparison of the shaped tubes with the shape of the vocal tract when making various vowel sounds, so you can see how the tubes match with what we're doing when we produce natural speech sounds.

Scan here or go to http://www.exploratorium.edu/files/exhibits/vocal_vowels/vocal_vowels.html to try out Exploratorium's 'Vocal Vowels'

Another fun online tool to help you get an idea of how the vocal tract works while you try to synthesize sounds is Pink Trombone's 'bare handed speech synthesis'. Manipulate the shapes of the oral cavity and see what kinds of sounds you can produce.

Scan here or go to https://dood.al/pinktrombone to try out Pink Trombone's 'bare-handed speech synthesis'

These days, speech synthesizers tend to be one of two kinds: concatenating, which string together recorded words and phrases; and those which use statistical methods and machine learning to generate speech from individual speech sounds. There are also systems which combine these two types of synthesis together.

You can hear the concatenating ones all over the place, a very simple example being the automatic announcements you get on trains in many countries, including the UK. For concatenating systems to work—to sound natural, in other words—there has to be a good match between the speech in the different parts of the message. If this match is absent, it can sound rather disjointed, and even some of the best TTS systems still sound rather stilted.

I have a favourite example which always gets the intonation wrong in one particular place. On the service which goes between Waterloo and Reading, the announcements tell you which train it is, list all the stations the train will be calling at, what the name of the next station is, and what the name of the station is when you are just arriving into it. So, we've got (e.g.):

1. This is the A service to B.
2. This is the A service to B, calling at C, D, E, F, and B.
3. The next station is (e.g.) C.
4. This is (e.g.) C. Please remember to take all your belongings when leaving the train.

Key:

A = station of origin.
B = station of termination.
C, D, E, F = stations along the route.

There are other announcements (e.g. 'Alight here for G'; 'We are arriving in B. This train terminates here'), but the ones you hear most often are similar to those given above.

What we've got here is basically framing sentences, with the station names inserted where I've given letters. There are two recordings of each station name, depending on what kind of sentence it is and where the station names are inserted. Where the station name appears at the end of a statement or the end of a list, the intonation on it goes down. Where it appears as a non-final item in the list, the intonation has a fall-rise tone. For example (hear the sound files on the companion site):

- This is the Waterloo service ⬊⬈ | to Reading. ⬊ |
- This is the Waterloo service ⬊⬈ | to Reading, ⬊ | calling at (abbreviated list) Clapham Junction ⬊⬈ | Richmond ⬊⬈ | Sunningdale ⬊⬈ | Bracknell ⬊⬈ | and Reading. ⬊ |
- The next station is Richmond. ⬊ |

So far, so good.

The problem comes when you are in one of the intermediate stations—number (4) on the list above. As the first part of (4) is a statement of fact, the name of the station should have a falling tone on it. E.g.:

a. This is Sunningdale. ⬊ |

However, whoever has programmed the announcement software has chosen the fall-rise version of 'Sunningdale'.

b. This is Sunningdale. ⬊⬈ |

This has the effect of sounding rather surprised, like you're putting a question mark after the name of the station. It's like the train announcer wasn't expecting to be in Sunningdale.

c. This is Sunningdale? Oh no! I've missed my stop!

Well, I always have a good chuckle at this, anyway.
But I digress.

Assistive communication devices and bespoke voices

Frankie's husband feels the tears come to his eyes and a sob build in his throat. For years, since Frankie was diagnosed with locked-in syndrome and lost the ability to move and communicate verbally, Paul has heard her 'speak' through a machine with a synthesized voice which did not fit her—an off-the-shelf voice which made Frankie hesitant to use the computer program, as it simply wasn't representative of who she was. Neither of them thought so.

Now, after long months of work with researchers and voice specialists, and a voice sample donation from her slightly older sister, Frankie has a voice which is her own. It sounds like who she is: a thirty-three-year-old woman, bursting with life. It is remarkably close to her original voice. It seems like a miracle.

Frankie listens keenly to her new voice. She feels elated. Lifted. Represented. She feels like she has herself back again.

Frankie looks up at Paul with a gleam in her eye. Paul used to describe her as 'a right chatterbox' but, since the stroke resulted in locked-in syndrome, she has felt compelled to keep her conversational contributions to a minimum because of her mismatched voice. People would look around when she was 'speaking' and not realise the comments had come from her. With this voice, nothing will stop her!

Whatever modern scientists were building TTS synthesizers for, it soon became pretty clear that they could be used to help people like Stephen Hawking to have a voice. Speech synthesizers which enable people with no voice to speak are known as 'assistive communication devices'. There have been a number of different companies producing devices over the years, from desktop computer-based ones to hand-helds, and from those which involve using input from typing to those which react to muscular action—like Hawking's—to those which scan the eyes and work from gaze, like the ones used with sufferers of locked-in syndrome. As they tend to work relatively slowly compared with natural speech—one report suggests it typically took Stephen Hawking one minute to produce fifteen words, whereas with natural speech the typical rate is around 150 words per minute on average—many have a set phrase such as 'Please be patient with me while I compose my message' that users can activate. We have come on leaps and bounds in what is possible technologically speaking, but we are still not quite at the stage where the device reads brain activity and produces speech with the same speed as is possible among typical adults.

I mentioned earlier that Stephen Hawking's TTS synthesizer had a voice with an American accent. Over the years, devices have come into production which have a range of voices to more accurately reflect the speaker, but the choices are still fairly limited. If you are a fourteen-year-old British girl, for example, you may not want a synthesized voice which sounds like a thirty-something American man. The limited number of options may mean that, if you meet someone else who is also using an assisted communication device, they are using the same voice as you. As the voice is such an important part of someone's identity, this can be frustrating for both individuals and—indeed—even upsetting.

Recent developments in assistive communication device technology are trying to deal with this issue. The Proloquo2Go app,[13] for example, has a range of accents to choose from, as well as children's voices. At a conference in 2016, I watched an inspirational keynote presentation from Rupal Patel, the founder of a company which develops bespoke voices for those who are unable to speak. What the company does is take information about the vocal tract of the client, or a close family relative of the client, and—where possible—vocalizations the client is able to make, and uses computer modelling of that vocal tract and the available vocalizations to create a voice. This has the benefit of producing something unique for the individual and—as the client also has input into the process—something they can feel really belongs to them.

Currently, this kind of service is extremely niche and probably rather expensive. But again, speech scientists are looking into how this can be made more accessible by taking advantage of social media and the continually improving computing power and storage available to us today. In Patel's conference presentation she explained how, previously, voices used in assistive communication devices were either fully synthetic and not very natural sounding, or based on the voices of actors or other professional voice users. This is what limits the possible voices available. Patel's company, VocaliD, is using crowdsourcing to collect donated voices from thousands of speakers from a variety of countries and all walks of life. This enables them to match donor voices to the client and to select the aspects they need in order to produce synthesized speech which is a much better fit for the client. Patel has spoken about what VocaliD is doing on a number of platforms, including giving a talk at TED Women in 2013.[14] There's also a short video by VocaliD which gives examples of how the technology is impacting on real people.[15] It also shows how it impacts on the people around them—their families and friends. Your own voice is unique, and signals 'this is me' to those listening to you. That can mean as much to the people around you as it can to you as a speaker.

If you're interested in trying some TTS synthesizers, there are lots of free ones available online. Simply search for 'text to speech' and select from the results. They are also available on smartphones, and can be used to translate either spoken or written messages into other languages. We're not quite at the point of the Babelfish from *The Hitchhiker's Guide to the Galaxy*, or Star Trek's universal translator ... but we're getting there.

CHAPTER 7

English voices, global voices

t is the 2018 Miss Universe competition in Muang Thong Thani, Thailand. Women have come from all over the world to represent their countries; friendships are made and rivalries abound.

To satisfy the world's hunger for news of the event and of certain individuals, some contestants take to social media to document their behind-the-scenes experience. Among them is Sarah Rose Summers, Miss USA.

As part of her coverage, videos on Instagram show Summers taking it upon herself to pass judgement on the linguistic abilities of some of the other contestants. The main issue is whether or not they are able to speak English. Of Miss Vietnam, Summers comments: 'She pretends to know so much English and then you ask her a question after having a whole conversation with her and she goes [confused nod and smile].'[1] She then expresses sorrow and consternation at the shocking discovery that Miss Cambodia doesn't speak any English at all. 'Poor Cambodia,' Summers concludes. There is praise for fellow contestant Valeria Morales Delgado, Miss Colombia, who also appears in Summers's video. 'You do speak great English,' Summers says, with obvious approval.

Linguistic complacency thus rears its ugly head in the beauty industry.

In one horrified comment on the Instagram post, Summers is castigated for demonstrating 'normalized xenophobia', criticized for being condescending and intolerant, and reminded that she is taking part in a competition hosted in a country where English is not the main language.[2] The global media picks up on the story, and Summers is exposed to the kind of publicity she evidently did not want.

Tail between her legs, Miss USA apologizes. She was not a winner that night.

Native English speakers—particularly (but not exclusively) those from countries such as Britain and the United States—tend to assume that everyone speaks English. It has been described as the 'world's favourite language',[3] and is certainly the most widely spoken. But this situation has arisen for historical, political, and economic reasons, and not necessarily just because individuals are choosing English.

What I've written so far takes a rather British English-centric view of the voice and how people speak. I'm British English and I make no apology for writing about that. I've mentioned Scottish accents, and looked at American English in passing in Chapter 4, when I looked at singing in other accents and included an interview with an American DJ in Britain, Darren Redick. If you're interested in the differences between British and American English, I heartily recommend the work of Lynne Murphy, including her blog, *Separated by a Common Language*.[4]

This last short chapter looks at some of the issues of being an English speaker in places outside of England and Britain.

In my life as a researcher, one of the areas I spend time looking at is pronunciation in English spoken around the world. And it's not just accents and varieties. The whole thing can get very politically heated.

English, politics, and power

The English were not the only Europeans to travel around the world colonizing bits of it and creating empires. While there had been international trade routes going back before records began, a lot of European colonizing activity, led by the Spanish and Portuguese, took place in the 1400s and 1500s in what is known as the 'Age of Discovery'. Italian explorer Christopher Columbus, probably the most well-known figure of this period, discovered the Americas in 1492 under sponsorship from the Spanish crown—and largely by accident, it seems, as the story goes that he was looking for sea routes to Asia and thought if he kept sailing west he would land there. The English, French, and Dutch became increasingly envious of the burgeoning Spanish and Portuguese overseas empires and the wealth they were creating, and began to follow suit, setting up trade networks and establishing colonies of their own. There is some recognition now that English seafaring heroes such as Sir Francis Drake and Sir Walter Raleigh were probably involved in activity more closely associated with piracy than with mere innocent exploration.

English—and subsequently British—colonies included parts of the northern Americas, parts of Africa, areas of the Middle East, India, and what is now Pakistan, Singapore, and Malaysia, Hong Kong, and Australasia. Types of settlement and arrangements were different, however, with English speakers moving en masse to some areas (e.g. North America, South Africa, Australia, and New Zealand), whereas in others the situation involved small groups of people from the British governing classes moving overseas who were then involved mainly in governance, education, and the law (e.g. India, Hong Kong, Tanzania). Timings were also very different, with the last British colonies coming into being as late as after World War I.

Where the British moved en masse, and including the UK, we have what we call 'Old Varieties of English'—so the United States, Canada, and Australia are examples of this—whereas elsewhere English is spoken either as a 'New Variety of English' or as a second language (L2). Indian and Singapore English are usually given as examples of New Varieties of English, and places like Malaysia and Botswana have English as an L2. Where English is not spoken as an Old Variety of English, a New Variety of English, or L2, it is traditionally considered to be a foreign language (EFL = English as a Foreign Language); examples of countries having EFL speakers include Japan, China, Russia, non-English-speaking European countries, and most of those in the South American continent.

Where research is concerned, it is usual to talk about varieties of English around the world in terms of how they sound and what their grammatical structure is. Indeed, most of the work I have been involved with on English in Hong Kong, Malaysia, Vietnam, Japan, and Botswana has described aspects of speech rhythm and intonation, often in the context of language learning and multilingualism. For example, in Hong Kong, Cantonese is the first language (L1) of most speakers of English, with Standard Spoken Mandarin (Putonghua) as an additional second language (yes, you can have more than one L2), particularly since the return of Hong Kong to China in 1997. And the introduction of Putonghua to Hong Kong in 1997 was certainly a political move, if not a pragmatic one.

Something which there is less recognition of—or perhaps less willingness to talk about and recognize—is how English and its speakers have had an effect on peoples and cultures in the countries which made up parts of the British Empire. This effect is not always positive.

What you do see is criticism of the 'poor English' spoken by people from around the world who are not speakers of Older Varieties.

Let's start by looking at the issue of 'poor English'.

In 2002, I was invited to run a week-long workshop for trainers from an Indian call centre. The call centre serviced a lot of clients in the UK, from banks to technology support to mail order retailers, and the trainers had been sent to me for intensive training on pronunciation, particularly intonation. I was able to put together a package which also involved colleagues who came in to speak about British cultural issues and how they differed from an Indian context. We had an interesting week.

One of the things which came up was that the operators in the call centres—the people who actually answer your calls—were being accused of rudeness. This was leading to the customers complaining that they couldn't understand the operators, ostensibly because the operators' English was 'bad', but basically because the customers didn't want to have to deal with someone with an accent they weren't used to. Customers perceived the call centre operators as being 'foreign', unwilling to deal with them politely and had pretty much decided they were not going to understand the operatives' speech. They had decided that the English of the operators was 'poor'. The trainers hoped that by addressing some of the language issues which were causing the operators to sound rude to the British listeners, they would have less of a problem with customers deciding they simply couldn't understand the operators' speech and hanging up, dissatisfied.

There are a number of issues here. One of them is accent prejudice. We've already considered this in a British context... although I did not include issues of race and ethnicity in the discussion in Chapter 2. The accent Multicultural London English is an example of a home-grown British variety of English influenced by people from different races and ethnicities, and— as with any accent of English—it has its critics, as well as being an area of fascination for socio-phoneticians working on urban varieties in the UK.

Where speakers of New Varieties of English or L2 Englishes from other countries are concerned, there are also huge amounts of prejudice from some listener groups. Some of this is because these speakers are outside of the 'tribe', i.e., they are different, and different is perceived as threatening. Some of it is because, historically, British people (like other European colonizing powers) have been used to seeing themselves as superior to the colonized, and so anyone with an exotic accent is viewed as being morally and intellectually deficient in some way. And some of it is a matter of ignorance about how language and culture work in different parts of the world and how this might affect the way someone from outside of the UK speaks English. There is evidence of both ignorance and assumed superiority in the way Miss

Figure 17   Climbing head pattern

USA described Miss Vietnam's apparently clueless reaction to being asked a question in English.

One thing which came up with my call centre trainers was a particular intonation pattern which means something different in British and Indian English. We call it a 'climbing head' pattern, and it's shown in Figure 17 (hear the sound file on the companion site).

In General British English, this pattern is usually only used when the speaker is admonishing someone for showing a lack of intelligence in a particular situation, or has repeated something several times and is getting fed up with the interlocutor for not responding. It is called an 'emphatic head' pattern, and is used to show a kind of emphasis. Consider this exchange:

A: I can't get my computer to work.

B1: [Genuine question] Have you tried to turn it on?

A: It's not even showing a 'stand-by' light.

B2: [Repeated question—maybe A didn't hear me] Have you tried to turn it on?

A: I can't understand it. It's worked before.

B3: [Slowly and carefully] Have you tried to turn it on?

A: What??

B4: [Slowly, carefully, and emphatically—why isn't A listening??]: Have you tried to turn it on? ← climbing head

By the time we get to B4, speaker B has asked the same question four times and A has not responded. B is showing exasperation with A . . . and using intonation to do it.

In Indian English, this pattern does not indicate exasperation. It's a fairly common pattern which can be used in the opening of a conversation and, therefore, quite neutral. But, if it's used at B1 above, and if A is a listener who is not used to the Indian English pattern, it can sound like B is already making the assumption that speaker A is an idiot.

There are two (possibly more) ways to look at this.

On the one hand, if call centres are servicing a particular speaker group, it is reasonable to suggest that it is necessary to train operators to modify the way they speak in the direction of patterns in the target speaker group. This can ensure exchanges go smoothly and no assumptions are made about the attitude of the operator, particularly if the customer is likely to infer from the intonation that the attitude is negative.

But there's another side to this.

The fact that people in countries all over the world speak English is the legacy of colonialism. The British (and other European powers) invaded and colonized countries with very little thought about the full extent of the impact of this on the colonized. It was assumed by the colonizers that contact with Europeans could have nothing but a positive effect—and that was only if the Europeans were bothered about the effect on indigenous peoples. After all, the main aim of colonization was to increase the global power, wealth, and influence of the colonizing country.

From a linguistic point of view, the focus on the part of the British seems to have been that English should be imposed on the colonized peoples in order to enable them to meet European cultural, moral, and intellectual standards. These standards were not sensitive to existing standards and socio-cultural practices. Some might well ask whether this has changed among speakers of Older Varieties of English. Miss USA's unfortunate comments provide some evidence that it has not.

One well-known narrative account of why English should be used in order to impose British values on people in the British Empire is the 'Macaulay Minute'. Thomas Babington Macaulay was a Whig politician in the 1800s who played a key role in the introduction of English language education in India. The Macaulay Minute, written in 1835, discusses the merits of using English as opposed to Sanskrit and Arabic. In it, Macaulay claims that Western literature is superior to any written in Sanskrit or Arabic, that English is 'better worth knowing' than Sanskrit or Arabic, and goes on to state the following:

We must at present do our best to form a class who may be interpreters between us and the millions whom we govern, -a class of persons Indian in blood and colour, but English in tastes, in opinions, in morals and in intellect. To that class we may leave it to refine the vernacular dialects of the country, to enrich those dialects with terms of science borrowed from the Western nomenclature, and to render them by degrees fit vehicles for conveying knowledge to the great mass of the population.[5]

In order to achieve this, that class 'who may be interpreters' between the British ruling classes and the Indian people were to be educated in English at the expense of Sanskrit and Arabic.

So, where am I going with this, exactly?

Given this oppressive linguistic history, speakers of Older Varieties of English are basically extremely lucky that English is the global language. Personally, I am amazed that people still want to speak it. But they do want to speak it—and increasing numbers want to speak it. For example, English has recently been adopted by the Association of Southeast Asian Nations (ASEAN) as its working and official language; member countries are Brunei Darussalam, Cambodia, Indonesia, Laos, Malaysia, Myanmar, the Philippines, Singapore, Thailand, and Vietnam, several of which have nothing to do with the British Commonwealth.

What we should be doing (in my opinion) is realizing that we are living in a world where English does not belong to speakers of Older Varieties any more—but speakers of Older Varieties benefit, often disproportionately, from the fact that English is spoken. The British have become just one group of speakers of English in an extremely linguistically diverse Anglophone world, but regrettably the fact that English is the almost *de facto* second language of choice globally removes from speakers of Older Varieties of English the perceived burden of learning other languages. It perpetuates the notion among speakers of Older Varieties that it is not necessary to develop a good understanding of social and cultural practices across the world, something which is facilitated by learning and using other languages. And this lack of language learning among monolingual English speakers is not a good thing.

Just as negative attitudes towards speakers of other British accents are based on prejudice and stereotypes, and negative attitudes towards features of women's speech are basically couched in male chauvinism, the assumption that a non-Older Variety speaker's speech is 'poor' simply because they are 'foreign' is based on attitudes which are stereotypical rather than factual. And what about the argument that these speakers of English are too difficult to understand? I have heard many British English speakers whose speech was unintelligible; the inability to be clearly spoken is not an inherent feature of speakers of New Varieties or L2 English.

Something that it would be useful for the British to be mindful of is that English would probably not have its standing in the world today were it not for the rise in economic and political power of the United States since World War II. Had the United States not taken its place on the world stage as it did, the linguistic situation around the world would most probably be rather different.

But English in the United States has its own challenges.

'Talking white'

In 2014, a YouTube video made by an African American woman using her phone went viral. It was on the topic of 'talking white'.[6]

In it, the speaker claims that there is no such thing as African Americans 'talking white', and that it is actually 'speaking fluently' or 'speaking your language correctly'. She says that in many cultures the ability to speak your language eloquently is admired, and is a mark of education. She laments the perceived prestige among some African Americans of sounding like they have no better than a 'fifth grade education', and says that it seems to her that African American culture frowns upon 'personal evolvement', the way that a person speaks being a symptom of that. Having 'proper diction' is not something that belongs to the Caucasian race, she says.

As I mentioned earlier, I have not looked at race or ethnicity in this book in any detail. This is a bit of a minefield for me, I feel. When I attended a conference on World Englishes several years ago, I heard from my Hong Kong and Singaporean colleagues that there was some interest in what I was doing there because I was viewed as some kind of representative of the former British Empire. Interesting, given I was there to speak about the development of English as an emerging New Variety in Hong Kong, and not the imposition of British English norms. The fact that

I compared British and Hong Kong English in my presentation was seen as an affront by some delegates, who inferred that I was upholding British English as an aspirational target of some sort.

When this issue of 'talking white' came up, I was wondering whether to write a blog post about it, but decided it was probably not my place to do so. I was invited on to local radio to talk about the issue in broader terms, and tried to stick to general things about language attitudes and how we make assumptions about people from the way they speak.

The woman in the video appeared as a guest on the radio show via Skype audio, and it turned out that her background was quite complex. She had emigrated to the United States from Kenya in her early teens, when her parents had relocated there. So actually, she wasn't African American. She was being judged by African Americans born in the United States, who saw somebody who looked like them—and therefore made all kinds of assumptions about her socio-cultural background—but didn't sound like them. They may have thought she was rejecting them by not using the linguistic features they associate with their cultural identity. She, in turn, was not brought up within that culture, and so her linguistic background was different.

Fascinating. And not too far removed from the hypothetical example of Alison Davies in Chapter 2, who had seemingly eschewed her Liverpool origins by changing the way she spoke to sound closer to SBS, much to the derision of social commentators.

What we have in the 'talking white' debate is a whole load of historical socio-cultural baggage that I can't even begin to identify with as a white British person. The British enslaved Africans and transported them in horrific conditions to work in equally horrific conditions miles away from their families, friends, and places of origin. English was forced upon them. It really isn't that much of a surprise that speaking the language like a white person, or 'talking white', is anathema to many African Americans.

My colleague Erhan Aslan and his co-author Camilla Vásquez have written about a related issue which went viral on the Internet in 2016.[7] A 13-year-old white American girl, Danielle Bregoli, appeared on the American talk show *Dr Phil* using language and speech which was perceived as African-American Vernacular English (AAVE). Her mother, who also appeared, did not use the same spoken features. The majority of comments on the YouTube footage of this interview, and the subsequent Internet meme, perceived Bregoli's speech negatively, some as unacceptable white appropriation of AAVE—e.g. 'white girl trying to sound black'; 'If you're not black, you can't speak our language'—and others saying she was not speaking 'proper English'. Talk show host Dr Phil himself asks her if she went to the fifth grade in school. This is an interesting comparison with the 'talking white' video, in which the black woman complains that she's being criticized for not using AAVE and instead speaking like a white person. She also implies that she believes using AAVE is perceived as an indicator of a poor education, referring to the fifth grade. Dr Phil's comments, and others in the data Aslan and Vásquez looked at, would seem to support that.

There is plenty more to be said about language, culture, and identity where race and ethnicity are concerned. Have a look at the section on further reading if you're interested in following this topic up.

'English makes me feel like a different person'

I want to end with an anecdote about how English can be a positive thing for speakers of New Varieties and for L2 learners.

What I've talked about so far all looks rather negative. But there are, of course, advantages to speaking English, and they can be more to do with personal identity than simply using it as a tool to get on in the world.

My colleague Jennifer Jenkins is well known for her work on English as a lingua franca. This paradigm initially included only people for whom English was not an L1 communicating in English with others for whom English was also not an L1. In recent years it has come to include any form of English used as a lingua franca, which might also include L1 speakers, but the focus is not on speakers of Older Varieties providing any kind of 'norm'. English is viewed as a truly global language, developing in a way to suit the communicative purposes of everyone who is using it.

In the course of this research, Jenny discovered that speakers of English actually felt liberated by it in some ways, as opposed to using their mother tongues. It helped them show aspects of their identity they had either not thought about before or had had to keep hidden for various linguistic and/or cultural reasons.

There is one example of this that particularly struck me from a young Japanese woman who was a student of mine at Reading several years ago. Japanese language and culture can be quite confining for women; the language has specific feminine forms used only by women, as well as masculine forms used only by men, and there is an expectation that women will speak in a particularly high-pitched, soft voice. Things are changing in Japan, but linguistic and cultural aspects are always slow to evolve. When I described pitch as being a sociolinguistic marker in Japan in my class the other day, another female Japanese student queried this with me, but then admitted this high-pitched, soft way of speaking for women is still regarded favourably in Japan.

When we were talking about language and identity in my *English in the World* class several years ago, the Japanese student sat quietly and listened to the discussion. She then put up her hand to make a comment. She said that she felt she was more able to be herself when she was speaking English. We had been reading about this in the text book, written by Jenny;[8] the Japanese student told me she suddenly realized that she was indeed able to show a different side of her personality when using English, that it was a side she was more comfortable with for expressing certain things, and that English released her some-how from the requirements of sticking to her Japanese cultural norms in more ways than simply having to sound feminine when she spoke.

This was a bit of a revelation to her at this time. I watched as she sat in the class and processed these thoughts.

I have to admit, I like these moments.

So, what have we learned?

In this book, I have attempted to throw some light on why it is that we are judged instantly by the way that we speak, and how one's speech is an intrinsic part of that person's individual and social identity.

There is plenty to say about English in the British Isles, but English is not only spoken there—and it's not the case that only English is spoken there either.

The English language itself is of rich mixed heritage; it is constantly changing, easily influenced by other languages, and this has affected—and continues to affect—the way it is spoken.

The way we speak develops from what we hear around us, and has the ability to reflect one person's identity, but also their multiple identities, depending on whom they are speaking to, what they're doing, or where they are. It can point to group identities, and signal affiliations and allegiances. It can deliberately single a person out, for good or bad.

Whether we like it or not, we are judged on the way we speak: on our accent, our voice quality, our pitch, our ability to enunciate clearly. There is probably no language of which this is truer than English—certainly in present times, with its position as a global language.

For some, this book may raise more questions than answers. As far as I'm concerned, if I've got you thinking about the way you and other people speak, what that says about us, and what we infer, consciously or otherwise ... that's a good thing.

To paraphrase Stephen Hawking: Let's keep talking.

Further reading

This is a very short annotated bibliography of accessible books you may find interesting if you'd like to follow up on any of the issues I've discussed here. There's much more out there than what I've listed below! And several other publications I've referred to in this book that might interest you. But this is a good place to start.

Aitchison, Jean. (2011). *The articulate mammal: an introduction to psycholinguistics* (5th Ed.). London & New York: Routledge.

I talked about child language acquisition of speech sounds in Chapter 1. Jean Aitchison's book is the first one I read on psycholinguistics as an undergraduate, and I found it to be an absolute page-turner. She explains things beautifully. If you're interested in how the mind processes language and how babies and children acquire their first language, give it a try.

Crystal, David. (2018). *Sounds appealing: the passionate story of English pronunciation.* London: Profile Books.

There surely isn't anyone more prolific on the topic of the English language than David Crystal. I'd recommend you read any book of his, but this one is particularly good for a highly accessible introduction to how spoken English is produced and pronounced. And, as with every book written by David, it's entertaining too.

Fisher, Jeremy, and Gillyanne Kayes. (2016). *This is a voice: 99 exercises to train, project and harness the power of your voice.* London: Wellcome Collection.

I'd been wanting to write the book you're now reading for some time. My experience at the *This is a voice* panel event in 2016 really galvanized my desire to write it. The book accompanying the exhibition is written by two vocal coaches, and aims at helping the reader get more from their voice from a performance perspective by understanding how it works and then knowing what to do with it. Whether you're an actor, singer, or just want to speak more clearly, you'll find this book useful. Your voice is you. Nurture it. Love it. Protect it. Develop it.

Jenkins, Jennifer. (2007). *English as a lingua franca: attitude and identity*. Oxford: Oxford University Press.

If you're interested in how English is taught and spoken around the world, how it is judged, and what it means to the people who speak and teach it, look no further than this fascinating book by Professor of Global Englishes, Jennifer Jenkins. Coming originally from an English Language Teaching background, Jenny is a world-leading authority on how people communicate internationally through the medium of spoken English. Her book draws on research conducted among teachers worldwide, and is a revealing account of what it is like to be a non-native speaker teacher of English.

Murphy, Lynne. (2018). *The prodigal tongue: the love-hate relationship between British and American English*. London: Oneworld Publications.

As I mentioned earlier, I haven't gone into American accents in a big way in this book, other than considering why people sing in an American accent or chatting with Darren Redick about his voice. If you're looking for an extremely informative, entertaining, and well-researched book on British and American English—including numerous references to pronunciation—look no further than this. Lynne is a lexicographer, an American in Britain, and has been blogging on this subject for years. She is one of the most entertaining and engaging speakers I have seen on this topic. And she makes a really good case for her claim that America saved the English language.

Roach, P. (2001). *Phonetics*. Oxford: Oxford University Press.

One of a series of introductions to language study, Peter Roach's book is more technical than Crystal (2018) or Fisher and Kayes (2016), but written with his usual knack of making the area accessible and enjoyable. This book also gives an annotated bibliography of more technical readings, so it's worth having in your collection if you're thinking you might want to pursue study in this area.

Wells, John C. (1982). *Accents of English* (3 vols). Cambridge: Cambridge University Press.

In this ground-breaking three-volume set, John Wells describes his Standard Lexical Sets for English pronunciation, and then goes on to document British and global varieties using his framework. The Standard Lexical Sets have since been adopted by researchers all over the world for their work on accents of English.

List of figures and QR codes

Figures

1. The speech chain
   From Denes, Peter B., and Elliot N. Pinson. (2012). *The speech chain: the physics and biology of spoken language*. Pickle Partners Publishing, p. 5. Reproduced with permission.

2. Age of acquisition of English speech sounds
   From Williamson, Graham. (2010). 'Age of acquisition of speech sounds', *SLTinfo*, https://www.sltinfo.com/ess101-age-of-acquisition-of-speech-sounds/, accessed 17/09/2018. These norms are a compilation of three studies: Sander (1972), Grunwell (1981), and Smit et al. (1990). Compiled by Williamson (2010).

3. The organs of speech
   From Roach, Peter. (2001). *Phonetics*. Oxford: University Press, p. 21. Reproduced by permission of Oxford University Press from *Phonetics* by Peter Roach, H. G. Widdowson. © Oxford University Press 2001.

4. Map of England showing the Anglo-Saxon Kingdoms and Danish Districts, produced *c.*1909
   Image from http://www.gutenberg.org/ebooks/48451 Chapter IV, accessed 12/04/2019.

5. Rhotic and non-rhotic areas of England in the 1950s
   From Leemann, Adrian, Marie-José Kolly, and David Britain. (2018). 'The English Dialects App: the creation of a crowdsourced dialect corpus', *Ampersand* 5, 1–17. For colour maps, see also https://www.cam.ac.uk/research/news/cambridge-app-maps-decline-in-regional-diversity-of-english-dialects, accessed 29/09/2018.

6. Twitter exchange showing stereotypical denasalization among DJs

7. Sarah Walker's continuum of voice control

QR codes

Note: the external links that the QR code images lead to, as well as all other external links, were last accessed and found to be working on 24 June 2019.

URLs for the material appearing as QR codes in the book, along with other interesting links, sound files, and colour versions of some images, can be found on the companion website www.oup.co.uk/companion/setter

Acknowledgements

First, a thank you to the people who were interviewed for this book, or who took part in research that I've been involved in and have written about: singers Nicole Allan, Nadie Keating, Andrea Ojano, and John Mitchell; radio personalities Darren Redick, Ian Danter, and Sarah Walker; Mary the voice coach; my transgender friend Sophie and our other transgender interviewees, Matt, Christine, and Karen—and student Iona Jacob for collecting and analysing some of that data. Thanks also to others who either asked not to be named or whose names I've changed.

I've had great support from my colleagues Rodney Jones and Erhan Aslan for the writing of this book—particularly Erhan, who gave useful comments on draft chapters during a very busy time at work and personally. Thanks also to others who have read chapters, including Gabriella Corbani, who read Chapter 1 and encouraged me to keep going, and my father-in-law, Ian Morris, who read the whole thing and declared it fascinating and erudite (the old smoothie!).

I'd also like to mention warmly the support from the ever-patient Julia Steer and the attentive Vicki Sunter at Oxford University Press, and the encouragement from David Crystal. Thank you all.

I would not be where I am today without the support and instruction of inspirational phonetics colleagues, particularly Aileen Bloomer for introducing me to phonetics, Peter French and Marion Shirt for spotting my potential, John Wells for inviting me to work on the UCL Summer Course in English Phonetics (sign up!) and for his comments on the manuscript, and last but not least, Peter Roach: teacher, mentor, collaborator, friend.

Acknowledgements

Penultimate thanks go to my husband, Stuart Morris, for inspiring me to flout convention and write a book that cannot be entered into the UK Research Excellence Framework exercise. What a liberating exercise it has been! I hope it helps show that academics do have something to contribute outside of those ivory towers.

For my final thank you, take a look at the Epilogue which follows.

Epilogue

Dear Dad,

This book is all your fault.

I was going through some old documents last week and came across some pictures of you in uniform during the Second World War. This made me wonder what you'd make of my life now had you still been alive. OK, so you'd be over 100 if you were alive at the time I'm writing this so it's unlikely you would still be here...but you never got to see the adult I've become, and will never know how you've influenced my path or chosen profession.

It was you and Mum, you see, who got me interested in how people speak. Mum, through her love of musicals, introduced me to Eliza Doolittle in *My Fair Lady*—and who could not help but be captivated by Audrey Hepburn in that role? The beautiful (ostensibly) Cockney lady with the soot-smudged cheeks and dirty, ragged clothes, selling flowers on the steps of St Paul's Church, Covent Garden, who forthrightly grasped the opportunity to better herself by changing the way she spoke. Admittedly, she had to go through rather a lot of chauvinistic rubbish at the hands of Professor Higgins to make the change, and completely lose touch with her original social group, but it was a change she wanted. Near the end of the film, when asked how she can support herself without the help of the supreme master who is Henry Higgins, she says in a self-assured way, full of confidence, 'I'll teach phonetics'. That was the sort of independent woman I wanted to be...and maybe—just maybe—that phrase stuck with me.

It was you, Dad, who always picked me up on the way I spoke. I used to think you were just being a fussy old fart but, now I know more about you, I understand that you saw the way a person speaks as a way to a better life, and it had very little to do with movie representations like *My Fair Lady*, even though your life mirrored that to some extent. You had been born into a working-class household on the Old Kent Road in south London before the First World War. You were the middle one of nine children, and left school aged eleven to work as a barrow boy in Covent Garden Market. But you didn't stay there. As a very young man, you subsequently went to work as a bank clerk, and the documents I found with the pictures include testimonials to your trustworthiness and diligent work during that inter-war time. To get that job at the bank, you must have paid special attention to the way you spoke, just as the fictional Eliza Doolittle had to do to aspire to her vision of being a lady in a flower shop. You knew that how you speak has a direct influence on how people see you and, subsequently, how well you get on in life. Plus, you'd be a representative of the bank to the public, so had to be suitably spoken to convey the right image. Someone with an urban south London or Cockney accent simply would not have got the job.

My teachers suggested I might like to apply to study linguistics at university rather than English literature (thank you, Mr and Mrs Amos—very perceptive), and this can only have been through observations that I had analytical skills and noticed things about language. You encourage me in that, Dad; you made me analytical about speech. While doing my degree, I was introduced to the study of phonetics proper, which just made sense in a way that few other subjects ever had and is still a source of everyday fascination to me . . . and the rest is history.

So thanks, Dad, for helping to make me the person I am today. For giving me an ear for speech sounds and an eye for detail. For being the inspiration for this book. I hope you and Mum would be proud.

Your daughter ~ Jane

Endnotes

Chapter 1

1. I'm not recommending this practice!
2. Mampe, Birgit, Angela D. Friederici, Anne Christophe, and Kathleen Wermke. 'Newborns' cry melody is shaped by their native language', *Current Biology* 19.23 (2009): 1994–7.
3. Savage-Rumbaugh, E. Sue. (1986). *Ape language: from conditioned response to symbol.* Columbia, OH: Columbia University Press.
4. Aitchison, Jean. (2011). *The articulate mammal: an introduction to psycholinguistics.* London and New York: Routledge.
5. Berko, Jean, and Roger Brown (1960). 'Psycholinguistic research methods', in P. Mussen (ed.), *Handbook of research methods in child development.* New York: John Wiley, pp. 517–57.
6. Cruttenden, Alan. (2013). *Gimson's pronunciation of English.* London and New York: Routledge.
7. Jones, Daniel. (2011). *Cambridge English pronouncing dictionary.* Cambridge: Cambridge University Press.
8. See the excerpt from the Alan Titchmarsh Show on YouTube here: https://www.youtube.com/watch?v=mCWa8xEZ52g&t, retrieved 07/09/2018.
9. Wells, John C. (1982). *Accents of English* (Vol. 1). Cambridge: Cambridge University Press.
10. Content words include nouns (naming words—e.g. *cat, imagination*), main verbs (doing words, e.g. *walk, think*), adjectives (words which describe nouns, e.g. *pretty, grey*), and adverbs (words which describe verbs, e.g. *slowly, unhelpfully*).
11. Truss, Lynne. (2004). *Eats, shoots and leaves: the zero tolerance approach to punctuation.* Harmondsworth: Penguin.

Chapter 2

1. See https://www.theguardian.com/science/2018/feb/07/first-modern-britons-dark-black-skin-cheddar-man-dna-analysis-reveals, accessed 07/09/2018.
2. https://notendur.hi.is/haukurth/norse/articles/pronunc.html, accessed 07/09/2018.
3. https://www.youtube.com/watch?v=rbOSL0_Vs3c, accessed 07/09/2018.
4. Baratta, Alexander. (2018). *Accent and Teacher Identity in Britain: Linguistic Favouritism and Imposed Identities.* Bloomsbury: London.
5. https://www.independent.co.uk/news/uk/home-news/teacher-told-to-sound-less-northern-after-southern-ofsted-inspection-8947332.html, accessed 07/09/2018.
6. Ofsted is the English education standards watchdog.
7. Giles, Howard. (1970). 'Evaluative reactions to accents', *Educational Review* 22.3: 211–27.
8. https://www.independent.co.uk/voices/love-island-snobbery-class-northern-accents-audience-southern-a8415471.html, accessed 07/09/2018.

Chapter 3

1. Hughes, Susan M., Justin K. Mogilski, and Marissa A. Harrison. (2014). 'The perception and parameters of intentional voice manipulation', *Journal of Nonverbal Behavior* 38.1: 107–27.
2. https://debuk.wordpress.com/2016/03/12/the-taming-of-the-shrill/, accessed 07/09/2018.
3. https://www.wework.com/creator/start-your-business/ux-user-experience/say-it-like-you-mean-it-breaking-the-uptalk-habit/, accessed 07/09/2018.
4. https://www.youtube.com/watch?v=kIAmqXF6bBE&list=PLBJxx2dHkll7FG8kD-LzWJfdFse69lmA5, accessed 07/09/2018.

5. Roach, Peter. (2009). *English phonetics and phonology: a practical course.* Cambridge: Cambridge University Press.

6. Cruttenden, Alan. (1997). *Intonation.* Cambridge: Cambridge University Press.

7. http://www.news.com.au/lifestyle/health/brits-are-banning-aussie-upspeak/news-story/7a67fec26215ebc9f6fcc73dbbbdfc94, accessed 07/09/2018.

8. https://www.spectator.co.uk/2014/02/warning-upspeak-can-dam age-your-career/, accessed 07/09/2018.

9. Warren, Paul. (2016). *Uptalk: the phenomenon of rising intonation.* Cambridge: Cambridge University Press.

10. http://time.com/2820087/3-speech-habits-that-are-worse-than-vocal-fry-in-job-interviews/, accessed 07/09/2018.

11. https://www.theguardian.com/commentisfree/2015/jul/24/vocal-fry-strong-female-voice, accessed 07/09/2018.

12. Yuasa, Ikuko Patricia. (2010). 'Creaky voice: a new feminine voice quality for young urban-oriented upwardly mobile American women?', *American Speech* 85.3: 315–37.

13. http://www.slate.com/blogs/lexicon_valley/2014/12/16/uptalk_is_okay_young_women_shouldn_t_have_to_talk_like_men_to_be_taken_seriously.html, accessed 07/09/2018.

Chapter 4

1. You can hear Alex Ferguson's [ɾ] in this clip from the television game show, *Who Wants to Be a Millionaire* (at 07.35): https://www.youtube.com/watch?v=1bgU2_3DQks, accessed 07/09/2018.

2. https://www.youtube.com/watch?v=HhP7T3n6DAU&t=115s, accessed 07/09/2018.

3. https://www.pri.org/stories/2015-11-10/faking-funk, accessed 07/09/2018. Quiz from 03:00.

4. https://www.cam.ac.uk/research/news/cambridge-app-maps-decline-in-regional-diversity-of-english-dialects, accessed 07/09/2018.

Chapter 5

1. The names and the accounts of any criminal cases mentioned here are fictional, based on real events.
2. https://www.york.ac.uk/language/postgraduate/taught/forensic-speech-science/, accessed 14/09/2018.
3. http://www.nytimes.com/2006/08/01/science/01whis.html?_r=0, accessed 14/09/2018.
4. https://www.phon.ucl.ac.uk/resource/sfs/, accessed 11/04/2019.
5. http://www.praat.org, accessed 14/09/2018.
6. http://www.speech.cs.cmu.edu/comp.speech/Section1/Labs/kay.html, accessed 14/09/2018.
7. Population averages from Cruttenden, Alan. (2014). *Gimson's pronunciation of English*. London & New York: Routledge, p. 104.
8. Hudson, Tobias, Kirsty McDougall, and Vincent Hughes. (Forthcoming). 'Forensic phonetics', in Rachael-Anne Knight, and Jane Setter (eds), *The Cambridge handbook of phonetics*. Cambridge: Cambridge University Press.
9. See, for example, https://www.theguardian.com/technology/2018/may/16/yanny-or-laurel-sound-illusion-sets-off-ear-splitting-arguments, accessed 14/09/2018.
10. https://forensictranscription.com.au/laurel-yanny, accessed 11/04/2019.

Chapter 6

1. I have changed all the names of transgender speakers in this chapter with the exception of Sophie, who agreed to be named.
2. https://www.youtube.com/watch?v=lrYx7HaUlMY, accessed 14/09/2018.
3. https://www.youtube.com/watch?v=2ZiVPh12RQY, accessed 14/09/2018.
4. Wong, Sidney Gig-Jan. (2017). *Exploring the vocal satisfaction and self-perceived vocal masculinity of transmasculine individuals.*

MA dissertation, University of Canterbury, New Zealand. https://
ir.canterbury.ac.nz/bitstream/handle/10092/15492/Wong,%20Sid-
ney_MLing%20Thesis.pdf?sequence=1, accessed 14/09/2018.

5. Günzburger, Deborah. (1995). 'Acoustic and perceptual implications of the transsexual voice', *Archives of Sexual Behavior* 24(3):
   339–48.

6. Hillenbrand, James M., and Michael J. Clark. (2009). 'The role of f
   0 and formant frequencies in distinguishing the voices of men and
   women', *Attention, Perception, & Psychophysics* 71(5): 1150–66.

7. International Phonetic Association, The. (1999). *Handbook of
   the International Phonetic Association.* Cambridge: Cambridge
   University Press.

8. https://wellcomecollection.org/thisisavoice, accessed 14/09/2018.

9. Fisher, Jeremy, and Gillyanne Kayes. (2016). *This is a voice.*
   London: Wellcome Collection.

10. https://www.theguardian.com/science/2018/jul/12/the-real-
    reason-the-sound-of-your-own-voice-makes-you-cringe, accessed
    14/09/2018.

11. https://www.youtube.com/watch?v=Ogt-hT9Wzlw, accessed 14/
    09/2018.

12. Mehrabian, Albert. (1971). *Silent messages* (Vol. 8). Belmont, CA:
    Wadsworth.

13. https://www.assistiveware.com/products/proloquo2go, accessed
    20/12/2018.

14. https://www.ted.com/talks/rupal_patel_synthetic_voices_as_unique_
    as_fingerprints, accessed 14/09/2018.

15. https://www.youtube.com/watch?v=b6QhgQqxdew, accessed 14/
    09/2018.

Chapter 7

1. https://www.theguardian.com/us-news/2018/dec/14/miss-usa-
   apologizes-mocking-fellow-competitors, accessed 15/12/2018.

2. https://www.instagram.com/p/BrUHzaZlD9O/?utm_source=ig_ embed, accessed 20/12/2018.
3. E.g. https://www.bbc.co.uk/news/world-44200901, accessed 20/12/ 2018.
4. https://separatedbyacommonlanguage.blogspot.com/, accessed 01/ 10/2018.
5. http://www.columbia.edu/itc/mealac/pritchett/00generallinks/mac aulay/txt_minute_education_1835.html, accessed 01/10/2018.
6. https://www.youtube.com/watch?v=1wzwU7OWq2M, accessed 01/10/2018.
7. Aslan, Erhan, and Camilla Vásquez. (2018). 'Cash me ousside': a citizen sociolinguistic analysis of online metalinguistic commentary. *Journal of Sociolinguistics*, pp. 1–26.
8. Jenkins, Jennifer. (2014). *Global Englishes: a resource book for students*. London and New York: Routledge.

Index